SCOTLAND'S FORGOTTEN MASSACRE

by
Sandy
Mullay

MOORFOOT PUBLISHING
EDINBURGH   1979

Published by Moorfoot Publishing,
P.O. Box 506,
S.W. Postal District,
Edinburgh 10.

1979 © A. J. Mullay

Printed by Geo. Stewart & Co. Ltd., Edinburgh

ISBN 0 906606 00 4

CONTENTS

Sandy Mullay is a free-lance author and publisher who began this study as part of an Open University course.

The footnote numbers in the text refer to historical sources listed in Appendix I. The numbering sequence begins anew with each chapter. These notes supply only bibliographical information and are not intended to add to the information contained in the text.

INTRODUCTION

In a year which witnessed international warfare on an unprecedented scale and a rash of domestic rioting throughout Scotland, there occurred at Tranent, East Lothian, one of the bloodiest atrocities on the British mainland since the battle of Culloden.

Twelve villagers, most of them probably unarmed and including a boy of fourteen, were killed and up to twenty more injured by regular cavalry units. It is possible that the Prime Minister of the day, William Pitt, may have drilled the troops personally before they were sent to Scotland, and it is remarkable that the Scottish authorities went to some trouble to avoid prosecuting those responsible for the massacre. It is an incident which has been largely ignored by historians until recently and this book is intended to throw new light on what happened and suggest aspects of the subject requiring further research.

Before considering the Tranent Riot, the subsequent massacre, and the legal aftermath, it is necessary to reconstruct the background to the incident which opened with the passing of the Scottish Militia Act of 1797. This was the first link in the chain of events ending in the bloodshed of the 29th of August 1797.

The Reaction to the Scottish Militia Act, 1797

The outbreak of war with France in 1793 did not immediately create a need for a people's militia in Scotland. At the time there was no reason to believe that France would become so militarily dominant on the Continent that she might become a threat to Britain, and with so much civil unrest, the authorities feared that distributing arms to the population might reproduce the events in France four years earlier.

But by the beginning of 1797 the war in Europe had gone against Britain and her allies. France ruled the Continent, and her fleet, if combined with that of Spain, posed a threat to British security. So serious was the possibility of invasion that the authorities were forced to consider arming those who were unsympathetic to the government's anxieties — those who had not been among the volunteers who swelled the forces at the outbreak of war. An English militia had existed for home defence since the seventeen-fifties, but no similar arrangements were made for Scotland which, only some ten years before, had heard the beating of Jacobite drums. In 1797 the decision was taken to form a Scottish militia.

The Scottish Militia Act was passed in June, and called for a force of six thousand men to serve exclusively in Scotland, the length of service being restricted to the duration of the war and a short token period afterwards.[1] A scheme was also to be introduced to assist militiamen to set up in trade after the war and recruits were to be drawn only from men aged between eighteen and twenty-three. Nor was recruitment to be entirely compulsory. Young men in this age-group would, if not excluded by being married with more than two children, have their names included in a ballot. If selected, the ballotee could be excused service if he paid for a substitute.

Such were the recruitment terms, which appear mild by twentieth century standards when conscription has become an accepted fact of life in war and sometimes in peace.

The balloting arrangements called into action the network of county and deputy lieutenants. Lists of ballotees were to be based on the parish registers of those who had attended schools a few years earlier and were to be scrutinised at public meetings held by the deputy lieutenants at focal points in each county. Any man objecting to being included could do so freely, and the amended lists were then to be forwarded to the county's Lord Lieutenant who would send them on to London. During July the Act's conditions were publicised by the pinning of handbills to church doors and the publication of advertisements in the newspapers. Whether these measures were sufficient in informing the population of the Act's intentions and provisions is shown to be doubtful by the events of the next two months.

'The present opposition to the militia act was unforeseen and unexpected'.[2] So wrote the *Edinburgh Evening Courant* in August 1797 as almost the whole of Scotland experienced civil turmoil of a kind unknown since the end of the Jacobite Rebellion. From Kirkcudbright in the south to Aboyne in the north, violent reaction to the Militia Act flared throughout the country. And on the day that this issue of the *Courant* appeared, several people lost their lives at Tranent when the Act was being enforced.

The first signs of opposition to the Act appear to have come from the Borders. Around the 20th August[3] Berwickshire's deputy lieutenants, attempting to hold a public scrutiny of balloting lists at Eccles, were forced to sign a declaration promising to desist from carrying out their duty.[4] It was mob violence which forced the officials to back down; earlier, one of them had his farmyard set on fire.[5] On the 21st August the Cinque Ports Cavalry — who will figure again in this narrative — were sent to Eccles and arrests were made.[6] At Jedburgh on the 22nd,[7] an even more extreme riot broke out and the officer commanding thirty local yeomanry cavalry[8] was injured. Not surprisingly, on the same day, the Lord Lieutenant, the Duke of Roxburghe requested that military reinforcements should be sent from Edinburgh 'with as much expedition as possible'.[9]

Other Borderers were roused. The *Scots Chronicle* reported that a Selkirk crowd of up to eight hundred men had burned balloting lists on August 26th,[10] and had injured a Mr Scott, an official attempting to implement the Act. In the nearby parish of Bowden, 'Mr Tulloch . . .

of Edliston has been obliged to get from Kelso a party of dragoons, to guard his house night and day; the mob having threatened to duck him in his pleasure ponds'.[10]

The hostile reaction to the Act mushroomed in all parts of Scotland, and inevitably those whose duty it was to enforce it found themselves the objects of public wrath. It must have been particularly hard on the schoolmasters; unlike the deputy lieutenants they lived in the middle of the communities which felt aggrieved, and could not hope for military protection in carrying out their everyday work. Mr Tulloch of Edliston was not the only person threatened with a ducking that summer — the unfortunate teacher at New Cumnock, Ayrshire, was immersed in a loch to the point of death.[11] At Carstairs the schoolhouse was set ablaze[12] and the Cambusnethan schoolmaster, James Lockhart, was forced to sign a declaration promising not to assist in implementing the Act.[13] In Dumfriesshire some schoolmasters refused to co-operate in the administration of the Act, which is hardly surprising; the *Scots Chronicle*[14] of September 1st carried a report of a schoolmaster in the Fife village of Kettle being killed in a disturbance.

The strength of popular reaction brought a variety of responses from the next tier of administrators, the deputy lieutenants. At Bathgate around the 24th August, Lord Polkemmet, a Mr Marjoribanks, and Patrick Geddes 'voluntarily granted their bond (written on stamped paper in the local church) under penalty of forfeiting their estates, not to implement the Act'.[15] The mob which forced this concession from the West Lothian officials then crossed into Lanarkshire to confront James Lockhart, and this is a rare example of an organised and mobile group reaction to the new law. There were other examples of deputies deciding that discretion was the better part of valour when facing anti-militia demonstrators. At Moffat, Sir William Maxwell, Colonel Dirom, and a Mr Graham of Mossknow were made 'to sign obligation on stamped paper that they never would interfere in the business again.'[16] This attempt at quasi-official annulment of the Militia Act caused at least one observer some amusement, the London correspondent of the *Scots Chronicle* commenting:

> 'The people of Scotland, it appears, have bound down some of the Lord Lieutenant in the whole worth of their estates, that they shall not attempt to carry into execution the new militia act. This

is however but an *Irish* kind of business, for who will sue for the *penalty*?'[17]

Not all the deputies were to be intimidated however. The Sheriff of Peebles, Mr Wolfe Murray,[18] dispersed a mob, while near Kirkcaldy, at Raith House — home of a Mr Ferguson — rioters from Dysart and Linkton scattered after failing to persuade the local deputy, probably Mr Ferguson himself, not to arrange a balloting meeting.[19]

Even the uppermost tier of county administration, the Lord Lieutenantry, was vulnerable to the expression of hostile popular opinion. The Duke of Atholl, responsible for administering the Act in Perthshire, was confronted by the agitated tenants of his estates, and in the meeting which followed, it seems that the Duke agreed not to put the law into operation.[20] This announcement was greeted with celebrations in the local taverns and it appears that the reassured tenants prevented another mob of four hundred from reaching the Duke's seat, Blair Castle.[21] It may well be that the Duke merely agreed to temporise until it was seen whether the law would be enforced elsewhere;[22] but whatever his decision he certainly gave his deputies permission to adjourn troublesome meetings for up to fourteen days.[23]

Scotland's reaction to the Militia Act worried the authorities in both Edinburgh and London. Pressed by the Lord Lieutenants for more military assistance, Lord Adam Gordon — Commander in Chief, North Britain — asked for reinforcements from the south as early as August 23rd. His need must have appeared all the greater after receiving a report that Callendar House had been burned to the ground by Falkirk rioters — a report later discovered to be erroneous, despite eye-witness accounts.[24] Gordon's request was answered promptly. Within ten days he was able to tell the Home Secretary, the Duke of Portland, that

'three regiments of Light Fencible Cavalry and one battalion of Fencible Infantry, are on their march from Northumberland to us, and will be of infinite service'.[25]

Henry Dundas, 'Scotland's uncrowned king', lately moved from the Home Office to be Secretary of State for War, took what modern observers would regard as a 'hawkish' viewpoint. Writing to Robert Dundas, the Lord Advocate — who happened to be his nephew — he stated his belief that the local military forces were insufficiently strict:

'The yeomanry and every other persons are much mistaken if they think their barn yards or any thing else will be safer by timidity in taking care of themselves and their property'.[26]

He assured the Lord Advocate that he intended to press the Commander in Chief, the Duke of York, for more troops.[27] Writing to Portland, his successor at the Home Office, Henry Dundas went on to suggest the transfer of cavalry units from Ireland to Scotland, in particular to Dumfriesshire, 'where I am sorry to observe they on . . . accounts stand much in need of more aid'.[28]

As Lord Advocate, Robert Dundas held a post which made him responsible for the enforcement of the Act and the prosecution of those who opposed it unlawfully. With the creation of the post of Secretary of State for Scotland still some eighty years away, the Lord Advocate was the only Scottish member of the Cabinet and effectively the government's representative in Scotland. It must have been a demanding position to hold at such a time. Even before the Tranent Riot which was to absorb so much of his attention in the months to come, Dundas was clearly worried by the response to the Militia Act as reports flowed in during August and September of riotous meetings, intimidated deputies, and vacillating lord lieutenants. Writing later in September he said 'our magistrates begin to recover from the trepidation into which I was hurt and alarmed to see they had fallen',[29] but it is possible that this trepidation may have earlier communicated itself to Dundas. A letter he sent Portland on August 27th states:

> 'And till your Grace's answer is received, or till we are instructed here, to prepare for an Order in Council suspending the execution of the Act, a measure which some judge expedient and necessary',[30]

implying that Dundas himself regarded the suspension of the Act as a possible course of action. Portland, four hundred miles to the south, may not have shared Dundas's concern to the same extent. On September 4th he replied:

> 'Notwithstanding the necessity I feel for carrying the Act into effect, I am far from saying that it may not be very advisable to postpone the meetings in the most dissatisfied counties, until the measure has been more generally adopted in those, where the opposition to it is less, or more certain of being got the better of'.[31]

What an encouragement these letters — especially Dundas's — would
have been to the Act's opponents had they known their contents! For
the opposition to the law, although largely violent and uncontrolled,
also took the form of newspaper advertisements, usually in the *Scots
Chronicle,* petitioning the King to suspend the Act, a move which
Dundas regarded as potentially necessary. One example of this is the
advert placed by the parishioners of Denny, Stirlingshire, in the
Chronicle for 19th[32] September. The citizens of Denny declared their
intention to correspond with other parishes peaceably objecting to the
Act, but at the same time publicised their 'detestation of all riotous
and disorderly proceedings'.

But these public statements were few in number; the standard
vehicle for public protest was the mob. There may have been as many
as fifty mob actions protesting against the Militia Act and it is
remarkable that there appears to have been only one fatality — the Fife
schoolmaster at Kettle — apart from the Tranent massacre. The
mobbings themselves were unusual in that they appear to have been
genuinely popular movements, often well-organised, but not controlled
in the way that mobs sometimes were at the time, making them
political weapons in the hands of the powerful or the ambitious. 'The
employment of the "mob" . . . was an established technique in the
eighteenth century'; so writes the historian E. P. Thompson in his book
The making of the English working class.[33] There is little evidence of
exploitation in the history of the anti-militia mobs, although in
Lanarkshire one such mob's demands for the abolition of the horse tax
has suggested 'backing from men of substance' to another modern
historian, J. R. Western.[34]

Occasionally popular protest threw off the restrictions of burgh life,
and ambushes and chases occurred which would rival for excitement or
colour anything which took place against the French. One such
incident occurred on 24th August. According to the *Scots Chronicle,* a
mob at Barry, near Dundee, stopped deputies riding to West Haven
and an old woman threatened the officials with a 'spurtle' or porridge-
stick unless they gave up their papers.[35] This transaction might have
amused the paper's readers had not the same issue carried a report of
what had happened at Tranent. Whether the porridge-stirrer was later
brought before the courts is not apparently recorded.

A more serious incident took place in Perthshire. A party of
Windsor Forresters arrested two rioters at Weem, near Taybridge, and

proceeded along the Perth road with their prisoners in a coach. Their departure was not unopposed however. Up to five hundred rioters pursued them, firing as they rode. After a running exchange of fire the party arrived unharmed in Perth, the officer in charge being hailed as a hero by the *Caledonian Mercury* in its report of September 21st.[36]

An equally dramatic event took place in Dunbartonshire on August 25th. A riot began during a deputies' meeting at Easter Kilpatrick and the official party thought it prudent to withdraw, with the crowd following close behind. The deputies took refuge in Garscube House close by, hurriedly preparing for a siege while the demonstrators massed nearby, deliberating what to do. An ugly confrontation was averted by the sudden arrival of a force of cavalry riding hard from Glasgow; the crowd promptly broke up. The incident brought about no injuries but some arrests were made, those apprehended being tried in Glasgow on September 19th.[37]

To the modern reader a list of mob actions in towns and villages, chases on horseback along country roads — even of deputy lieutenants ambushed by an old woman wielding a porridge-stick — prompts the question 'why?' Why were the Scots so reluctant to form militias for service in their home areas, particularly when there was such a real threat of foreign invasion? Was there a nationwide aversion to the political establishment of the time; a feeling that if the French were installed in Westminster and Edinburgh, this might be a change for the better? Certainly, Henry Dundas, Pitt's War Minister, advised Portland the Home Secretary that 'Jacobism' was 'at the bottom of it'.[38] However, this may have been a typically extreme view from an arch-Tory; the correspondence among the ruling elites of the time shows more concern with controlling Scotland's unrest than in understanding it.

Significantly, during the second month of the disturbances, Dundas's nephew Robert, the Lord Advocate, was striving to clarify the conditions of militia service. In a letter of September 6th he recommended to Portland the circulation of a handbill written by the Sheriff of West Lothian to remedy public misunderstanding of the Militia Act.[39] This notice emphasised the condition of domestic service and the limited chance of ballotees actually being conscripted, which suggests that the authorities believed these to be crucial points in the public's reaction to the Act. A similar message was published by the Duke of Buccleuch in the Edinburgh newspapers in late August.[40]

These steps were probably taken in the light of reports received from deputies dealing with angry protests against the Act. From the historian's point of view one of the most informative letters preserved in the public archives is one sent by two Dumfriesshire deputies, William Kirkpatrick and Henry Veitch, to their Lord Lieutenant, the Duke of Queensberry. This letter,[41] dated 31st August in the village of Closeburn, was passed by Queensberry to the Home Office and must have provided interesting reading. For the first time someone in authority was trying to understand the anti-militia riots.

Kirkpatrick and Veitch believed that to carry out the Act 'we humbly conceive, to be impossible.' On the practical level it appeared that not all rural parishes possessed schoolmasters to make up the lists of eligible men, while some of the dominies were reluctant to do so for fear of public reprisals. As to the disturbances themselves, the writers were in no doubt that a complete misunderstanding of the Act's conditions was the basis for national unrest. In particular, the promise of domestic service did not seem to be appreciated.

> 'In some places they are impressed with a notion, that the moment they are raised, the men are to be sent out of the Kingdom, to the East or West Indies . . . and in their present temper of mind, tho an angel were to come down from Heaven, he would not be able to persuade them to the contrary'.

This attitude to military recruitment was not peculiar to Dumfriesshire at this time. In his book *Britain and her army, 1509-1970,*[42] Correlli Barnett points out that

> 'between 1793 and 1796 the taking of French sugar islands cost the British army no fewer than 80,000 men, of whom 40,000 died and the rest were rendered unfit for service. This was a higher mortality than in all Wellington's (later) campaigns in the Peninsula'.

He goes on to say

> 'once the mortal nature of a posting to the West Indies dawned on the British lower classes . . . the West Indies became a major deterrent to recruitment'.

This suggests that there was a need to fully explain the condition of domestic service, although there are two complications possibly worth considering. Only three years earlier there had been mutinies in the newly-raised Fencible regiments in Scotland when it was proposed to send them for service in England or further afield. This was regarded as a breach of a recruitment condition and rumours of it may not have been forgotten by those not yet in uniform. Similarly, there may have been a belief that militias would eventually be used as manpower reservoirs for the regular line regiments — a suspicion proved to be largely correct in later years.

Kirkpatrick and Veitch had discovered other reasons for popular distrust of the military authorities. In six Dumfriesshire parishes no fewer than seven hundred able-bodied volunteers had been rejected for military service, then, following the passing of the Militia Act, it appeared that they were to be 'pressed' into service, 'for in this light they see the matter'.[43] The inference to be drawn was that the army wanted recruits — but on its own terms.

Finally, the method of selecting recruits, the ballot, was unpopular. Although at first glance this would appear to be a fair method of selection, and one which ensured that not all young men would be drafted, there was a common fund of sympathy for those whom fate picked.

> 'Both the young men themselves, and their parents, consider as a sad grievance, that they should be liable to be carried off, while nine times their number, every way as fit for the purpose, are exempted.'[44]

On hearing this complaint the authorities may have wearily concluded that there was to be no pleasing everyone, but in the eighteenth century, popular opinion was not something the government usually took into its consideration.

> 'Haldane of Gleneagles remarked that the people nowadays expected to have everything explained to them "so far has the spirit of democracy prevailed"'.[45]

So writes J. R. Western; he goes on to say

> 'This was true: the riots of 1797 subsided when the authorities began to explain the scheme properly'.

Looking back on the events of August and September, the ruling elite probably realised that earlier efforts to explain the purpose of the

militia and the method of raising it might have saved a great deal of
military activity which could have been more usefully employed against
the French. Such efforts might also have reduced the Tranent incident
to nothing more than a name in a list of militia riots instead of
producing a stain on Scotland's history.

Gradually, with the circulation of more information about militia
conditions, protests diminished. On September 19th Portland sent to
Robert Dundas

> 'my congratulations, on the prospect which every day's
> intelligence opens more fully and satisfactorily of a speedy
> termination of all the difficulties with which the measure of
> raising a militia was threatened'.[46]

But the last word on the national problem of enforcing the Militia
Act should be left with the Duke of Roxburghe. Writing to Portland on
September 2nd he found it necessary to explain the sorry performance
of the local yeomanry during the violent Jedburgh riot ten days
previously. He pointed out that

> 'their arms were not ready to be delivered to them 'till the very
> day on the which the Riot happened at Jedburgh, (so) it cannot
> be expected that they should as yet be perfect in the use of
> them . . . The corps is composed chiefly of opulent farmers,
> whose long absence from home during the harvest would be
> almost ruin to them. The populace as yet hold them in contempt
> as soldiers, but they dread the appearance of the dragoons'.[47]

'They dread the appearance of the dragoons'. Roxburghe seemed to
have been so distant from the 'populace' that he wrote about them as if
they were the enemy. When facing the Tranent rioters, the dragoons
may have felt the same.

Tranent

Tranent is an East Lothian town half way between Edinburgh and Haddington, at about ten miles distance from each. The town crowns a limestone ridge running east and west and looks down on the Firth of Forth a mile to the north. At this point the Edinburgh-London road turns inland from the coastal strip, crosses the ridge, and heads south-eastwards towards Haddington, the county town.

Tranent has always come under the administrative wing of Haddington, the 'Lamp of Lothian' nestling in the rich agricultural land in the centre of the county, but Tranent, in the north-west corner, seems isolated from it. The community has been a mining centre for centuries and is the largest burgh in East Lothian.[1] Although only a few miles from Edinburgh and Haddington, it is almost as if Tranent is widely separated from them both; from Edinburgh, which in the seventeen-nineties was Scotland's largest city and possibly Europe's most intellectually distinguished, and separate from Haddington in its contrasting life-style.

From its height Tranent overlooks the Battlefield of Prestonpans, where in 1745, the Jacobites under Bonnie Prince Charlie routed a government army and sent Johnny Cope fleeing south. The battlefield was bisected by a wooden waggon-way built as early as 1722.[2] This allowed loaded coal-trucks to roll downhill to the port of Cockenzie where the coal was shipped to other areas unable to boast such a modern transport facility. Tranent seems fated to mix its military and industrial histories.

Coal was first worked in this area in the thirteenth century by the monks of Newbattle Abbey, but even a century earlier the Tranent parish church is first mentioned in the records as having been donated to the Abbey of Holyrood, suggesting a sizeable community in the twelfth century.[3] By the seventeenth, coal mining — a process of picking at the surface where the coal seams were accessible — was practised, and the local aristocrat, the Earl of Winton, 'was reputed to be the greatest coal and salt master in Scotland'.[4] In 1715 however, a significant change occurred. For supporting the cause of the Old Pretender, Winton had his estate confiscated by the Crown, and it came into the possession of a commercial firm, the York Buildings Company. This had two long-term effects. Firstly, the coal industry in the area intensified. 'With the coming of the York Buildings Company new methods were introduced and lower seams were worked for the first time'; so says the *Third Statistical Account* of the parish.[5] It was the company which pioneered the use of the waggon-way, and employed steam-power for draining the Tranent pit as early as 1719.[6] This was only twelve years after the Treaty of Union, only four since the first Jacobite Rebellion. Tranent tasted the Industrial Revolution early.

The second effect of Winton's punishment was the removal from the area of an aristocratic employer and patron, and the importance of this will be seen later.

A glance at the map on page 23 provides evidence of the industrial development of Tranent and its environs. In the seventeen-nineties, three pits were being operated, although the York Buildings Company had been bought out by the Cadell family around 1779.[7] The pits at Tranent, Elphinstone and Birsley employed a considerable proportion of the village's 2,500 population, where there was a ratio of four miners to every weaver, weaving being the industry next to mining in importance.[8]

It would be wrong to assume that Tranent was totally dependent on coal-mining. Unlike the inhabitants of later mining villages which mushroomed around giant pits, the Tranent villagers were also active in other occupations. The parish contained a tannery, a nail-making firm and a distillery with its own small coal-supply at St Clement's Wells. Weaving was important, with some weavers doing 'what is called factory work'. This description from the *First Statistical Account*[9] probably implies 'putting-out', a practice which enabled the operative to work a loom in his own home with the help of his family. Raw material would be supplied by the textile company, which might also be the owner of the loom, making the weaver dependent on the company to a considerable extent. But at least the worker could follow his own schedule, 'able to stop the loom just when he chose in order to speak to a neighbour', as T. C. Smout, the leading social historian, has pointed out.[10] The factory system had not then taken on the awful soul-destroying character that it was to assume in the next century.

Agriculture completed the employment spectrum. It was reputed that land to the north of the village was the best in quality, possibly cultivated in strips by such workers as the weavers, who at the time almost certainly ranked above the colliers. To the visitor, it is likely that the landscape around the town showed extensive cultivation with pock-marks of coal-workings dotted here and there, and the wooden rails running down to the sea.

Writing his *Statistical Account* in 1793, the parish minister, the Reverend Hugh Cunningham, said: 'A considerable proportion of the parishioners either belong to or are connected with, the collieries'.[11] 'Belong to' are not words used idly in this context.

Coal-mining was one of Scotland's first industries, but after developing early, entered a period of technological stagnation until new mechanised working methods appeared late in the nineteenth century. Tranent, with its steam engines and waggon-way, was among the more modern coal-producing areas in the seventeen-nineties, but the laborious method of digging out the coal was still dependent on the brute strength of the miner.

> 'The miners themselves went on hewing in the nineteenth century with exactly the same tools as their ancestors had done two hundred years before'.[12]

Not only was the job strenuous, it was also downright dangerous. The Tranent area was always considered 'wet' underground: as late as the nineteen-fifties the *Third Statistical Account* noted that 'previously a miner came home black, and often dripping wet'.[13] Flooding was a permanent danger, probably accounting for the early introduction of steam power to tackle the problem. Additionally, some of the coal workings were so shallow that miners underground could identify the arrival of the mail coach in the village from the sound of other vehicular traffic.[14] In such workings roof collapse would be a constant hazard.

But it was not only men who were exposed to these dangers. The Tranent colliers comprised men, women, and children, and the Lothian coalfield was one of the last areas in Scotland where whole families toiled underground. According to Smout,

'it was customary for the collier's wife or daughter to drag the
coal from the face where her husband worked to the foot of the
shaft, and then to carry it up the steep turnpike stair to the
pithead'.[15]

Smout suggests that this is the equivalent of a woman carrying one and
a half hundredweights of coal from Portobello to the top of Arthur's
Seat four times a day.[16] Nor were such feminine foibles as pregnancy
given much consideration. The 1842 commission on mine labour
interviewed a Tranent collier, Elizabeth McNeill, aged thirty-eight, who
said:

'Women think little of working below when with child; have
wrought myself till the last hour, and returned again twelve or
fourteen days after'.[17]

This mother of seven already had three of her children working as
colliers.

'I must confess that children are sent down too early, but it is better
for them than running wild about'. This was Mrs McNeill's opinion.

One ten-year-old Tranent collier, William Martin, told the
commissioners,

'I fa' asleep sometimes when we canna get the coals away, but the
shaft of my faither's pick soon wakens me up. The place I work
in the noo is wet; the water covers my shae-taps, and am obliged
to sit in it to work. Naebody takes anything but cake or bread
below, and we seldom change our clothes, as it is so late before
we get hame'.[18]

And when they got there, what was 'hame' to the Tranent colliers?
In his definitive work on Scottish social history, T. C. Smout pictures
the exhausted mother returning home to a cold house, possibly with a
baby to feed, and meals to prepare for the rest of the returning family.
Domestic conditions could hardly be anything but squalid, and the
1842 commission found that 'miners kept pigs, ducks and fowls in their
houses, drank spirits hard and ran into debt.'[19]

It is important to remember that this evidence was collected some
forty-five years after the Tranent riot; there is no evidence to suggest
that earlier working and living conditions were better; no reason to

doubt that life for the colliers was, in the words of Hobbes, 'poor, nasty, brutish and short'.

One possible reason for the lack of development in new mining methods was the existence of a cheap captive labour force, and 'captive' is almost literally true. In 1797 the Tranent colliers were still technically serfs owned by their employer, in this case the Cadell family. In theory an Act passed in 1775 had freed colliers from this bondage, but the measure had proved ineffective. The social status of colliers had always been lowly. In 1701 they had been excluded from a Scottish Habeas Corpus Act, while in some areas deceased miners could not be buried in consecrated ground, so isolated were they from the rest of the community.[20] This degree of ostracism was by no means universal, but, as Smout points out, East of Scotland owners probably worked their property — the colliers — hardest because of commercial competition from the richer coalfields of Northumberland and Durham, whose coal could reach Scotland by sea.[21]

A 1799 Act of Parliament was to free colliers from the miserable status of being slaves in their own country. It ended 'arling', a practice of committing children, even those unborn, to work for a particular owner, but did nothing to exclude women and children from pit labour. One later improvement in the Tranent area was that the Cadells were to offer their employees four-year contracts worth £6,[22] but this was after the Tranent riot; in 1797 it is likely that the colliers were still serfs.

Mineworkers were among the pioneers of trade union activity, and contemporary evidence of this can be gleaned from a 1793 publication, an Edinburgh pamphlet entitled *Considerations on the present scarcity and high price of coals in Scotland.*[23] To say that the anonymous author is prejudiced against colliers is to understate the case. After describing colliers as being 'destitute of all principles of religion and morality', the writer goes on to suggest that his enemy is well organised.

> 'They have among them what is called *brotherings*. It is a solemn oath, or engagement, to stand by each other. In the west country, where this practice is universal, they have some watch-word, by sending around of which they can lay the whole of the collieries in the country idle.'

Although referring to the West of Scotland, it is perhaps significant that in 1786 there was a strike at Elphinstone, only two miles from Tranent, suggesting some measure of trade union activity in the area.

However, the main impact of this pamphlet lay in its circulation among the upper and middle classes, and its probable reinforcement of existing contempt of colliers, with very little possibility of counter-propaganda being issued on the colliers' behalf.

Writing of the popular attitude to colliers in 1799, Lord Cockburn said in his *Memorials of his time,* 'the taste for improving the lower orders had not then begun to dawn . . . people cared nothing about colliers on their own account'.[24]

When facing the county officers and the dragoons, the Tranent rioters may have been conscious of this.

The Tranent Militia Riot

The Tranent riot of August 29th 1797 was one of many instigated by the enforcement of the Militia Act, but differed in one respect from the others. It incurred a death toll of twelve, while other disturbances were comparatively bloodless. We have already seen some of the factors which sparked off protests against the Act in other areas — fear of postings abroad in disease-ridden lands, apprehension about recruitment conditions following the army's refusal of many volunteers, and a sense of injustice directed against the ballot arrangements. Although these factors were present at Tranent, the riot there was more violent than any other and triggered off an atrocity as bloody as any in Scotland's chequered past.

Why was Tranent so different? A clue can be found in the dual nature of the historical evidence. Take for example two accounts of the same incident which occurred on the evening of Monday, August 28th, the eve of the riot:

'The first symptoms of outrage appeared on the evening of the 28th, when an orderly dragoon, riding through Tranent, was assaulted by the people with stones, and driven out of the town, on the supposition that he was carrying some message relative to the militia business'.

'On Monday evening, between eight and nine o' clock, a dragoon of the cavalry lying at the Barracks, and a Gentleman's servant in company with him, came riding through the town of Tranent, and two or three persons happening to be standing at their doors conversing together, were, without any provocation, suddenly attacked by the soldier on horseback, who, putting spurs to his horse, endeavoured to ride them; the people, however, kept him off; he then went away about twenty yards, when he returned, damning the people, who now took hold of his horse by

24

the bridle, and he then attempting to draw his sword, they seized upon the hilt and prevented him. This extraordinary behaviour drew the attention of several women and boys, who began pelting the dragoon with stones . . . This, it seems, had the effect to inflame the minds of the women and children in the town of Tranent, and, in a little while, a parcel of young lads and boys assembled in the street, huzzaing and waving their hats, crying out "No militia".'

The first version of this incident is taken from evidence given by Major Wight in a libel trial some twelve months after the event.[1] The second, and more detailed, statement, is from a newspaper published within a week of the event.[2] The latter report was accompanied by a fairly accurate description of the events of the 29th, including a realistic estimate of the number of dead. The historian is probably inclined to attach more weight to the latter evidence than to Wight's, but in doing so, he has made an unconscious decision. He has decided that historical records are always suspect, and, in this case, should be regarded as propaganda from two opposed factions. This is reasonable; the Tranent riot and massacre were largely the result of class differences, as the often opposing accounts of the affair show. Those Scots who like to believe they are the products of a traditionally classless society would do well to attach some importance to the Tranent incident in their vague recollections of Scottish history.

One factor common to both accounts is the atmosphere of expectation of the next day's militia meeting, due to be held at midday, when the balloting lists for all local parishes would be publicly examined. Whether the incident involving the dragoon was the stimulus of mob activity, or merely one phase in its progress, the fact was that the village was roused that evening.

There are reports of villagers marching from Tranent to neighbouring villages 'to the tuck of drum' as James Miller, the Haddington historian puts it.[3] Miller implies that the mobs intimidated everyone they met into protesting against the Militia Act, and Tranent seems to have been no different from other areas in that the unfortunate schoolmasters had to bear the brunt of the people's wrath.

The Tranent schoolmaster was Robert Paisley. Hearing the shouts of an approaching crowd and the pulse of a drum, Paisley slipped from his house into the summer evening and took shelter with the parish minister, probably Hugh Cunningham, from whose writings we know so much about Tranent. Faced with an excited crowd demanding the list of Tranent ballotees, Mrs Paisley handed over various papers and registers, but in place of the school register, she passed off another document in its place. Since most of the villagers were probably illiterate, and in any case too excited to trouble with details, this ruse appears to have fooled the citizens, who marched off in triumph. In fact the genuine list had already been deposited at Glen's Inn, where the next day's meeting was to take place. When Paisley returned home to his cool-headed wife — and we have no record of how she welcomed him — he decided to inform the deputy lieutenants of what had happened, and of the villagers' threat to burn St Germains, the home of David Anderson, one of the deputies. During the course of the evening, a mob did approach St Germains, but apparently turned aside at the last minute.[4]

Paisley's journey through the gathering darkness to St Germains earned him permission to absent himself from the next day's meeting, and Miller records that the schoolmaster was not seen again in the district for a month.[5] Nor was he the only schoolmaster to experience trouble. David Graham, the Saltoun master, had already been confronted by a village mob demanding that he surrender his balloting list. This he had bravely refused to do, but on the evening of the meeting he evidently decided to take no further risks, riding to Glen's Inn in Tranent and staying there overnight, where he was probably unknown. The Pencaitland master, a Mr Sanderson, was saved from the action of a mob by his parish minister,[6] while his Gladsmuir counterpart, Hugh Ramsay, was forced from his house. Ramsay, like Paisley, reported to St Germains.

An experience to rival any of these befell Alexander Thomson of Ormiston who was held up on the road the following day, and forced to surrender his list.[7] The evidence of this incident seems ambiguous; after mentioning Thomson's meeting with rioters, Miller goes on to relate that in fact the Ormiston list was later examined at the Tranent meeting.[8] Suffice to say that, as in other discontented areas of Scotland, the schoolmasters were in the front-line of public anger, and they appear to have responded with varying degrees of courage and resourcefulness.

Meanwhile at St Germains, with the shouts of colliers and the beat of drums echoing through the gloaming, David Anderson wrote a letter to Captain Findlay of nearby Drummore House, requesting 'a pair of horses and a postilion' to take his family away from danger the next day.[9] He also asked Findlay, the local commander of the Cinque Ports Cavalry — then at Haddington — for military assistance. This letter was sent at around ten in the evening, and was only one indication that there would be little sleep for the authorities as they prepared to tackle the villagers on the ridge above.

Anderson was a troop commander of the East Lothian Yeomanry Cavalry,[10] the members of which began to assemble at St Germains as dawn was streaking the sky. As they did so, they found that twenty-two of Findlay's Cinque Ports had arrived at about three in response to Anderson's request.[11] At around the same time, the other deputies arrived — fifty-seven year old John Cadell, the local coalmine owner, Andrew Wight of Port Seton, and Andrew Gray of Southfield. One prominent representative of military authority at the house that morning was the Commander in Chief for North Britain, Lord Adam Gordon, who had ridden from Haddington with some of Findlay's cavalry, but did not stay for the morning's events, continuing instead to Edinburgh.[12]

Another member of the 1797 elite who was absent, was Lord Hawkesbury, the colonel of the Cinque Ports. His lordship remained at Haddington where another militia meeting was scheduled for the same day.[13] This was to be a source of subsequent comment; one later witness arguing that Tranent was not the bed of rebellion it was reputed to be:

'The noble commander of the Cinque Ports, perceiving no appearance of disposition or disturbance, considered his presence to be unnecessary . . . leaving the command of the cavalry to a young gentleman, one of his captains'.[14]

Whether Hawkesbury plumped for the Haddington meeting instead of Tranent because he expected it to be quieter or because he felt that propriety demanded that he be present at the meeting in the county town, is immaterial. The fact is that a future British prime minister kept his name out of the Tranent affair.

As the daylight of August 29th broadened across the sky, the St Germains party must have taken stock of their preparations for the day's business ahead of them. The pressing need was for reinforcements to augment the forty cavalrymen present, half of them part-time soldiers, who, if the Duke of Roxburghe is to be believed, were unlikely to impress a determined mob. A letter was therefore despatched to Sir James Stewart, commander of the troops encamped at Musselburgh some three miles to the west, 'requesting that a detachment of one or two troops of cavalry might be sent to meet us at Tranent at twelve o' clock'.[15]

An additional precaution was taken by John Cadell, whose employees were expected to cause some degree of trouble. Cadell took with him a copy of the Riot Act, specially delivered from Haddington.[16] This Act of 1714 decreed that if a mob

> 'being required by a magistrate, by proclamation in the King's name, to disperse, shall nevertheless continue together for an hour after such proclamation, the persons disobeying shall suffer death.'[17]

Cadell probably believed that the public reading of this proclamation, coupled with his personal knowledge of his workforce, might render the presence of troops unnecessary.

According to Miller the official party left Anderson's house just after eleven, the cavalrymen riding first with the deputies bringing up the rear. As they rode up the muddy lanes through the belated harvest, they passed knots of women and children travelling in the same direction. Some of them shouted at the party, one woman advising Cadell 'take care of your head'.[18] Their route probably brought them into the village's narrow streets from the north-east, before they turned south and then east to Glen's Inn, the meeting place. (See map on page 23[19]).

Several things were happening at once. There was a barrage of shouts and jeering, but the deputies were fully occupied organising their military escort. It was thought politic to keep the soldiers away from the meeting unless their presence became urgently necessary. At the same time no fewer than eighty members of the Pembrokeshire Cavalry had arrived from Musselburgh under the command of Captain John Price.[20] They too were deployed on the edge of the village, and the deputies turned to face the gauntlet of villagers pressing on all sides as they pushed their way to the inn.

As they picked their way through the crowd Cadell and his fellow deputies heard the regular beat of a drum in the western part of the town, but they heard a lot more besides.

> 'One tall thin woman, the very prototype of Meg Merrilees . . .
> came running up to the head of the horses, holding out a great
> stone in her hand, and swearing that "she would have their hearts
> blood!"'

Another woman advised Cadell that he would have his brain knocked
out.[21] All this is from Miller's account of the incident and he goes on to
give the impression that the deputies were being harassed by enraged
women while their menfolk rallied in another part of the village for
later concerted action, implying a high degree of organisation.

Inevitably, there is another version. According to a statement made
in court during one of the subsequent trials

> ' . . . Mr Cadell, as soon as he entered the town of Tranent . . .
> and before having reached the inn, used various menacing
> expressions and gestures to the people, whom he met in the
> streets, and in particular to one man, whom he fiercely asked
> what was he doing there? and whom he wanted to lay hold of; but
> the rest of the gentlemen, with the constables and soldiers, did
> not stop for that purpose . . .'[22]

Once established in Glen's Inn, the deputies, having greeted the
waiting schoolmasters, wasted no time in getting on with the job at
hand. With Anderson appointed preses, or chairman, and the
Ormiston schoolmaster Alexander Thomson as secretary — no doubt
still shaken by his encounter with rioters on the road — the various
parish records were examined beginning with Humbie, and then on
through Saltoun, Ormiston, Prestonpans. According to Miller, Major
Wight went to the window of the inn, round which the crowd had
gathered, and explained to the assembled villagers how the meeting
would be conducted, the names of the parishioners liable to be
ballotted being shouted out, giving an opportunity for objections to be
made on grounds of age or marriage with two children
disqualifications.[23]

At about this point, the first stone was thrown.

Who threw it, and at what approximate time, are unanswered
questions. As Major Wight went down into the street to continue his
explanation to the crowd, the stone-throwing must have occurred later,
although as we shall see, there is evidence that one of the officials
actually threw stones *at* the crowd. However, from among the shouts of
'no militia!' Wight made out one rioter's suggestion that the deputies

should abandon the meeting, in which case they would be allowed to leave peacefully. The major confirmed the officials' determination to carry out their duty, in itself a brave decision; other militia-meeting officials, faced by smaller crowds than this, had made discretion the better part of valour. Those protesting at Tranent may have numbered two thousand, although contemporary estimates vary from three hundred to five thousand.[24] The deputies' only escorts at this time were probably a few constables, although one historian, Kenneth Logue, mentions the arrival of six cavalrymen commanded by a sergeant.[25]

Another peaceable suggestion put to Wight was that Scotsmen could not be drafted into a militia as this had never been done before, as it was 'against the Union'. This reference to the 1707 Act of Union was attributed to a collier named Duncan.[26] As it happens David Duncan was one of the rioters arrested during an incident at the other end of the village and Logue's account seems to suggest that this happened at about the same time.[27] This may appear to be an unimportant aspect of the whole incident, but it illustrates the confusion surrounding the riot, with many identities becoming confused. It is not even certain that the meeting was being conducted properly, and Logue has doubts on this point.[28] He believes that John Cadell was infuriated by the protests of the crowd and certainly there was no lack of witnesses later to condemn his conduct of the meeting.[29] Three people claimed to have seen the deputy lieutenant — a justice of the peace[30] — throwing stones at the crowd and push away one man who was attempting to make a reasonable protest against his name's inclusion in the ballot. This protester even claimed that Cadell had hit him on the head with his stick. Other witnesses were to make worse allegations about Cadell, which as Logue points out, he hardly denied in court.[31]

Here again, there is conflict in the evidence. Some of the more prominent citizens of this part of East Lothian were later to testify that Cadell had carried out his duties correctly and efficiently.[32]

However the meeting was being conducted, the turning point came with the arrival of Nicolas Outerside, presumably when there was a lull in the stone-throwing. After gaining entrance to the inn, Outerside presented the deputies with a document which on examination proved to be a 'round robin', a letter written in such a way that none of the names contained therein appeared at the head.[33] This was a sensible precaution in an age when sedition was punishable by transportation or worse, and the deputies may have considered the letter seditious enough. It recorded the disapproval felt by thirty Prestonpans villagers to the Militia Act and implied that, if enlisted, they would refuse to 'disperse our fellow countrymen, or to oppose a foreign foe'. It was the rejection of this document, and the dismissal of Outerside — whom the officials thought 'a remarkably stupid fellow', which marked the real beginning of the riot.[34]

As if by a prearranged signal, the women melted from sight leaving the street to the men who were armed with sticks and stones. This is Miller's description of what happened at this stage, although as Logue points out later court testimony shows that women were always present in the street — probably one was shot there. Logue refutes Miller's implication that the rejection of the Prestonpans letter was the signal for a *planned* attack. He believes that the resulting violence was 'due more to anger at the way the letter was rejected and the general attitude of the deputies'.[35]

A hail of stones now struck the inn as the villagers laid siege to the official party. With the windows shattering and missiles ricocheting into the building, the deputies and schoolmasters were forced to retreat to a back room. The platoon sent earlier by Findlay attempted to drive back the crowd by rearing and prancing their horses, but the situation was too violent for such an exercise to be effective.

Reinforcements of regular cavalry were by now attempting to relieve the besieged group, but soon realised that the rioters had gained a considerable strategic advantage by occupying the rooftops and by throwing missiles, including parts of the chimney-stacks, down on the advancing cavalry. The Cinque Ports and the Pembrokeshires managed to ride along the street firing with blank ammunition but even this failed to lift the siege of the inn. The horsemen must have been fully occupied in protecting their heads from stones and bricks, while the blank firing may have persuaded some villagers to believe that the soldiers were not prepared for a full-scale fight.[36] As it was, the cavalry action was ineffective and to make matters worse, Captain Findlay was unhorsed and had his sword stolen. The recovery of this sword is a complicated historical puzzle.

Robert Mitchell had travelled to Tranent to claim that he was over the age-limit for militia balloting. He was hiding in a house on the High Street to keep out of harm's way when the street action became violent. During the cavalry charge, a sword was thrown in the room

where Mitchell was sheltering and shortly afterwards Captain Findlay
arrived to recover the weapon, promptly apprehending the unfortunate
Mitchell.[37] The latter's story was given to the Earl of Haddington a few
days later and was corroborated by evidence given at about the same
time by none other than David Duncan — the same Duncan who had
claimed that the establishment of a Scottish militia was against the Act
of Union, and whom Logue believes was arrested for making a
menacing gesture at Findlay in an earlier incident at the west end of
the village.[38] The confusion in this comparatively minor incident
suggests that the collecting and weighing of evidence has proved as
complex as the unfolding of the day's events must have been to an
onlooker at the time. Duncan appears to turn up again at a later stage
of Miller's account.[39]

While the soldiers were attempting to control the stormy village,
John Cadell was making his own efforts to pacify the rioters. His first
attempt to read the Riot Act at a window of Glen's was drowned by the
noise and probably made Cadell a target for the crowd's missiles.[40] He
attempted a second time without success and it appears that he finally
went through the ritual of reading the document out loud on the
internal stair of the inn, as the crowd outside threw their missiles and
shouted their protests.[41] He might as well not have read it at all,
although one witness later testified that Cadell had held up a paper in
view of the crowd, saying it 'would do for them'. Apparently he also
damned the Tranent women 'for bitches' and threatened to have them
all hanged.[42] Although this evidence was corroborated, it is difficult to
imagine Cadell's words being so clearly heard when his attempts to
read the Act had been stifled by the din of the crowd. In fact,
according to the deputies' own version of this incident, Cadell actually
made his way into the street at about this time and 'entreated of the
people for God's sake to disperse'.[43] It is amazing that such a localised
affair could produce such conflicting testimony.

As the cavalry desperately tried to staunch the attacks coming at
them from doors, roofs, and alleys, it must have seemed to the deputies
that the rioters were succeeding in holding the upper hand. Already the
riot had reached a more violent extreme than any other in the recent
outburst of anti-militia feeling, and the Tranent villagers appear to
have been determined to do more than simply register their protest
against the Act's implementation. This prompts the question, was it the
purpose of the rioters to kill the members of the official party, to

'batter them doon' as one source puts it?[44] It is unfortunate that none of the riot participants appear to have recorded their plans or objectives; the historian is left with the impression of a demonstration with no purpose other than the purely negative one of defying the law and attempting to kill its administrators. Be that as it may, it was while the siege of Glen's inn was at its height that the military started shooting to kill.

'The question who gave the order to fire remains open'.[45] Logue's statement is the only possible conclusion that can be drawn from the problem of who ordered the military to open fire with ammunition knowing that casualties would be inevitable in the narrow streets and alleys. The soldiers were in no doubt that the deputies had given the order, as was legally necessary before soldiers could open fire on a crowd. Lord Adam Gordon wasted no time the next day to write to the Home Secretary firmly laying the responsibility with the civilian officials,[46] while they, in their published account of the riot, implied that their question 'why don't they fire?' had been asked in an almost rhetorical sense.[47]

If there is doubt about the origin of the order, there was no doubt about its effect. Although the troops' first round of shots failed to make much impression on the rioters, the mob began to fall back from the inn.[48] More significantly, some of the cavalry were now able to move to the north side of the village in a manouevre to use their carbines against the rioters on the roofs.[49] This proved to be a turning-point in the military operation which so far had been bungled; the cavalry had been seriously disadvantaged operating in the village street and lanes where bricks and stones rained down on them.

William Hunter was one of the first to die. He was positioned on a rooftop almost opposite the inn, giving him an excellent target for his missiles but making him dangerously vulnerable when the dragoons began to return fire. McNeill describes Hunter being shot from behind:

> 'his body rolled down the foreside of the house, and was caught by three or four dragoons on the points of their swords. Thus ended the first serious act in the tragedy of that day'.[50]

It is possible that McNeill was correct in assuming Hunter's to be the first death — his prominent position would make him a threat to the cavalry and thus a priority target. The description of his body being transfixed on the soldiers' swords is probably fanciful and does not appear in the evidence. The Tranent incident was bloody enough without such trimmings.

George Elder and Joan Crookston were shot in the street where they may have been prominent in the riot, but even those fleeing were not safe from the soldiers, who now held the upper hand. Isabel Rodger, aged nineteen, was pursued by a soldier into a passageway of a house and shot dead. William Smith died on the staircase of a house opposite the inn, again possibly following a chase.[51]

Mercifully, not all the military action ended in fatalities, although the 29th of August must have gouged a scar on many local memories. One Tranent girl of sixteen, Janet Forsyth, had left her job of cutting the corn in a nearby field to 'see the fun' and experienced more than she bargained for. After being pursued by a dragoon she was shot in the shoulder, and despite recovering, she carried the bullet for the rest of her life.[52] Another Tranent girl, seventeen-year-old Mary Allan, was shot at by a soldier in a narrow passage. Miraculously, the bullet missed her and lodged in the frame of the door, but its intended victim had already fainted, an action which probably convinced her pursuer that she had been hit. In fact, a cut on her forehead was later found to be her only injury.[53]

The local historian Peter McNeill — who has been regrettably casual in naming his sources — also describes an incident where a number of colliers and their families travelled from Elphinstone to Tranent for the meeting, the men going to the inn and the women and children to a friend's house.[54] During the military action a party of dragoons passed the house and seeing a group of women at the door, detached one soldier to investigate indoors.

> 'The fellow expecting, it is supposed, to find someone hiding in the bed, drove his sword several times down through the clothing, in course of which a child was heard to shriek'.

This brutal action drew the wrath of one of the women, a Mrs Reid, who threw the soldier into the street, much to the delight of bystanders. However her young son David lost one of his little fingers 'severed at the second joint'. Reid is not included in the list of dead and wounded drawn up by the parish minister a few days later, but McNeill justifies the truth of his account by saying that Reid's mutilated finger was remembered in Tranent well into the nineteenth century. Certainly, there is nothing in the history of the Tranent riot to suggest that this kind of behaviour was uncharacteristic of the troops at the incident.

Meanwhile, no doubt fortified by the dramatic reversal in fortunes, the deputies began to emerge from the inn.[55] Anderson left the centre of the village, possibly to rejoin his yeomanry cavalry still on standby at the east end of the High Street — although one source says that he went west to Musselburgh for reinforcements[56] — but it seems that John Cadell and other officials did not wish to miss the opportunity of personally stamping their authority on the villagers.

Miller gives an account of how Cadell and Wight pursued a collier named Duncan (perhaps David Duncan again, although McNeill calls him John Duncan).[57] This is a strange incident. Miller describes the deputies chasing Duncan 'up a lane into a small stackyard, which was much crowded with people, who all of them seemed to have sticks and bludgeons in their hands'. One might assume that the deputies had run into a trap, but it appears that, on the contrary, Duncan felt trapped and turned on his pursuers. Does this mean that the well-armed crowd had no more stomach for a fight? It certainly appears that Cadell dominated this situation, personally taking Duncan prisoner. If all the testimony is to be believed, this was not to be the end of Cadell's violence.

As the constables were assembling the thirty-six rioters who had been arrested — all were marched to Haddington — military reinforcements were being sought from Musselburgh, possibly by Anderson. At around two o' clock in the afternoon, two companies of Sutherland Fencible Infantry were mobilised but may not have reached the trouble-spot until early evening.[58]

With order restored, Cadell was in the process of restarting the official reading of the balloting-lists and possibly letting the villagers know he was in charge again. As Logue writes 'Mr Cadell's temper does not appear to have cooled any',[59] and there is strong evidence that he used considerable violence towards a number of people, particularly Janet Hogg, whose face he is alleged to have dashed against the door of the inn.[60] The evidence suggests that Cadell may have struck at least three people during the proceedings, despite the declarations of members of the parish elite testifying to his good behaviour.

Logue is in no doubt about Cadell's misbehaviour during the riot, but admits that one later declaration rings false. This was the evidence supplied by Margaret Smith, claiming that Cadell had ordered Findlay's troops to "ride four or five miles round the country and fire on or kill every person they saw'.[61] A modern historian would distrust

this kind of statement as it fits the facts *too* exactly, indicating a
fabrication of evidence designed to implicate Cadell in the subsequent
killings, but this is only one example of the evidence given against the
colliery owner. If it could be established whether Cadell had been ill-
tempered from the start of the meeting, or had only reacted violently
after the military had restored peace to the village, our knowledge of
that August day's happenings would be considerably enhanced, and
less dependent on statements which are so extreme as to be akin to
propaganda.

The Tranent riot was over, but the Tranent massacre was already
taking place in the fields outside the village, even as the deputies
reseated themselves in the inn and began calling the names of ballotees
through the broken window to the sullen crowd. In a letter to the
Home Secretary the following day, the military commander in Scotland,
Lord Adam Gordon, pointed out that the military action taken to stop
the riot had been successful in allowing the civil authorities to complete
their business.[62]

This suggests that what happened next was not only atrocious, it
was unnecessary.

The Tranent Massacre

The Tranent massacre is difficult for the historian to describe. It is tempting to let the imagination have free rein, just as the cavalrymen allowed their horses, and write graphically of the galloping cavalry riding down fleeing villagers in the fields, stabbing, shooting, even beheading as they went. One can picture the frustrated soldiers breaking free from the authority of the civilian officials at Tranent and venting their wrath on what they must have regarded as the rebellious rabble of the mining village. They can be seen not only killing and wounding, but indulging in deadly games of make-believe, pretending to shoot a wounded man in the head, firing a pistol in the face of a woman so that the bullet missed and the powder burned her features. And doing all this confident in the knowledge that they would not be brought to justice — the law which would imprison or transport a child for stealing a loaf of bread, did not appear to apply to the gentlemen of the British cavalry.

The most tragic aspects of the Tranent affair are that imagination is not required to write such an account of what happened on that August day, and that the Scottish legal system turned a blind eye to the atrocity.

As soon as the besieged deputies had ordered (according to the soldiers' claim) that the military should fire at the rioters in earnest, Captain Price took a troop of cavalry north of the inn to gain a clearer view of those on the rooftops. Using their carbines, the soldiers had little difficulty in clearing the roofs of missile-throwers thus giving their colleagues military supremacy in the streets. This manoeuvre was apparently carried out at the discretion of Price himself — the Lord Advocate was later to report to the Home Secretary that no order had been given for such an operation.[1] Having achieved this objective the cavalry probably then had a new view of the village and of rioters in full flight from the gunfire. Whatever the immediate impetus for the cavalry's subsequent action, it was probably the success of this move which liberated the cavalry in the village from the frustration of playing second fiddle to working-class rioters and inspired them to put spur to flank with deadly effect.

The definitive version of the Tranent massacre will probably remain that of Ken Logue's in his article (see appendix I)[2]. His work shows considerable research on the primary records, mainly court declarations. Although these declarations were made in some cases up to two years after the event, they represent the best evidence to fill out the details of the melancholy lists of dead and wounded sent by the Tranent minister, the Reverend Hugh Cunningham, to the Lord Lieutenant of East Lothian on September 2nd.[3]

But the most significant point concerning the massacre evidence is its apparent one-sidedness. While accounts of the riot often lend themselves to two interpretations — and some totally contradict one another — the information existing about the subsequent massacre is depressingly straightforward.

According to the evidence, the main setting of the massacre were the fields to the south and east of Tranent.[4] It appears that the cavalry made a broad sweep on the eastern side of the village, the whole operation possibly lasting no more than fifteen minutes[5] with the soldiers riding at the gallop and stopping only when they caught up with stragglers or even innocent travellers who knew nothing of the riot. During this quarter of an hour attempts were made to recall the cavalry by bugle but there seems to have been no standard system of bugle calls for operations where more than one regiment was involved. The Cinque Ports apparently heeded recall signals from their bugler, which leaves us with the conclusion that the perpetrators of the Tranent massacre were the Pembrokeshire cavalry: as Logue points out, it is suspicious that none of their number were available to give evidence following the incident.[6]

The route of the main body of soldiers was probably in an anti-clockwise direction. Logue quotes one witness who saw the dragoons set off down the Ormiston road, that is, in a south-easterly direction, (see map on page 39).[4] The map showing the location where the supposed rioters were shot begins with Peter Ness immediately to the south of the village, continues with Stephen Brotherstone on the Ormiston road, and then follows anti-clockwise up to John Adam shot and stabbed on the Haddington road to the north-east. At least one party of cavalry then proceeded north-east to Adniston where they arrested some

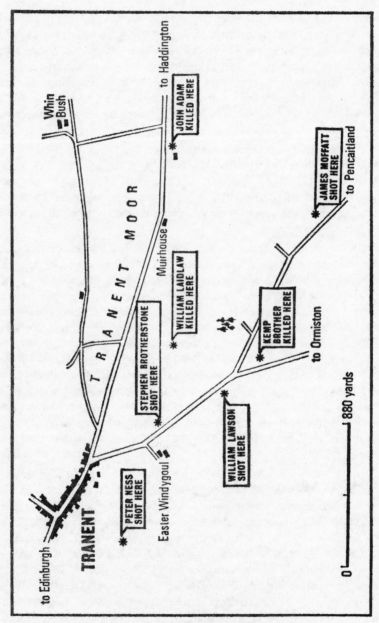

Drawing courtesy of *The Scotsman*

farmworkers who had just risen from their dinner, no doubt alarmed by the firing and the drumming of approaching hooves. This route is confirmed by Miller's mention of soldiers bursting into a house half-way between Adniston and Tranent, where, before returning to Tranent, 'they amused themselves . . . with holding the points of their naked sabres close to Mrs Carnegie's breast for several minutes'.[8] Although she could not have realised it at the time, Mrs Carnegie got off lightly.

It is academic to debate whether Peter Ness was the first to die outside the village or whether his body was simply the first to be discovered when the killings had ceased. Certainly he died comparatively close to the village within the sight of three witnesses, suggesting that the cavalry may have considered him as a rioter attempting to escape.

Ness had come to Tranent with a workmate, John Guild, to collect wages from his employer.[9] On arriving at the village they found Glen's inn besieged, but, according to Guild's later testimony, were not themselves involved in the riot. Sheltering in a house, they argued whether to remain there or leave the village. Ness decided to leave the house, not an unreasonable decision to make at the time. We have already seen how Robert Mitchell was arrested while he claimed to be innocently hiding from the violence of the riot, and both Isabel Rodger and William Smith appear to have been killed inside buildings. In the event, Ness made the wrong decision. While attempting to make his way round the south of Tranent he was chased by a number of cavalry, stumbled before they reached him, and was shot before he could rise. Later court declarations aver that he was shot again by a second soldier.

Next to die was a Pencaitland man, Stephen Brotherstone.[10] According to the evidence of his widow, the Brotherstones were making their way to Tranent from Pencaitland in the company of another Pencaitland villager, James Crichton, when they saw cavalry riding down the road towards them. The trio dived for cover behind a hedge, which the soldiers raked with gunfire as they passed. One of the troopers dismounted to view the results of this action and found that all three were alive. He began to attack Crichton — an unarmed elderly man — with his sword, before proceeding to hack at Brotherston's abdomen and legs. He then rode off, ignoring the distraught woman's pleadings. Surprisingly, neither Brotherstone nor Crichton were dead, but the former expired shortly after his wife had succeeded in borrowing a cart to transport him home. Crichton was listed as "dangerous" by the Reverend Cunningham in his letter to the Lord Lieutenant,[3] but in the absence of burial records for Pencaitland parish, it is impossible to know if his wounds were fatal.

On reflection, this incident on the road south-east of the village was remarkable in that those who suffered *were on their way* to Tranent and this must have been obvious to the soldiers riding down the road to meet them. It surely must have occurred to the dragoons that these people could not have been involved in the riot, and the brutality inflicted on them could only have been the action of men close to the border of psychopathy. The suggestion of the local historian, Peter McNeill, that the Pembrokeshires were drunk, seems an inadequate explanation, although such a suggestion emerged at one of the subsequent court hearings.[11]

Peter Lawson, further down the road, also had the perfect alibi for not being involved in the riot, in that he was on his way to the village.[12] Despite this, Lawson fared no better than had the Pencaitland three. Unlike them however, he does not appear to have attempted to escape from two approaching cavalrymen but explained that he was on route to Tranent with a load of wood. One soldier shot him 'upon his right side', knocking him to the ground. The second soldier then 'snapped (i.e. pretended to fire) his pistol three times at his head' as he lay on the ground. If the shooting of an unarmed innocent man was an act of pointless barbarity, the second soldier's action was inexplicably cruel.

Lawson's evidence was unique. He appears to be the only one of the Tranent casualties who was able to talk before he died and actually described his killer as having a scar on one cheek. In a later letter to the Home Secretary, the Lord Advocate showed his concern over Lawson's death, believing it to be unjustifiable.[13] However, there is no record that Lawson's murderer was ever charged, probably because of the opinion of Dundas's adviser, a London lawyer named Baldwin, who concluded that

> 'on the whole I cannot think it is a case which calls for a prosecution by government when the whole of the provocation is taken into account.'[14]

This incredible judgment is only one example of the double-think exhibited by the British administration of the time, since it must have been obvious that Lawson had offered no provocation at all. Another example was the Lord Advocate's belief that Brotherstone died on his way to join the mob, while Lawson, travelling in the same direction on the same road, had no such intention.[15] An additional turn in this fibre of twisted thinking was that anyone on their way to join a riot — which was unproved in the case of Brotherstone and Lawson — was considered just as guilty as someone who had taken part in one.

William Laidlaw's death is marked on the map, in a field half-way between the Haddington and Ormiston roads.[16] Laidlaw had been on the latter road with Alexander Robertson when they heard the drumming of hoofbeats — probably from the same group of soldiers who had despatched Brotherstone. In which direction the two were travelling is not apparently recorded, and there is even less information about the cavalry's action in this incident. Having left the road to escape the galloping dragoons, the two men ran through the fields, but their flight was hopeless. Robertson was struck twice by a dragoon, the first blow cutting his outstretched hand, the second rendering him unconscious. This may have given him the appearance of having died and probably satisfied the soldiers. It means however that we have no record of what happened to Laidlaw, whose bloodstained body Robertson later discovered lying not far away.

In eliminating D. Kemp, His Majesty's cavalry had the satisfaction of killing a thirteen-year-old boy who had come to Tranent thinking that the expected protest meeting might be a 'diversion'. He, (and the records do not appear to supply his Christian name[17]) and his younger brother William watched the riot from a safe vantage point until they decided, as Logue drily puts it, 'that it had become more than a diversion'.[18] On leaving the village, the youngsters found themselves pursued by cavalry and ran for their lives, separating at the fork of the Pencaitland and Ormiston roads. We know from William's subsequent testimony that he forked right and was overtaken by a dragoon who aimed a sword thrust at him. Mercifully, the blow merely cut off the top of a cane the boy carried and he was saved from further violence by the dragoon's inability to stop his horse, which galloped on.

William's elder brother was to have no such good fortune. His body was later found in a field between the two roads. He had been stabbed in the chest and the top of his skull was almost severed. 'nearly cut off from temple to temple'.[19]

Part of the *Scots Chronicle's* account of the massacre may relate to the boy's death:

> 'The cavalry rode through the corn fields, and gave no quarter; at the same time, some of their officers were heard to cry out, to shed no more blood; the soldiers dispersed in small parties, firing at those they came up with in the fields; a young boy was there killed, begging hard for his life'.[20]

Still the cavalry were not satisfied. One or two dragoons pursued James Moffatt in a field near the Pencaitland road, one of them firing and missing. A second soldier chased Moffatt and in doing so, lost his helmet:

> 'He called on Moffatt to turn back and lift it up, and he should receive no harm. Moffatt did so, and after delivering the helmet into the dragoon's hand, he turned about, and was going away, when the dragoon fired his pistol or carbine at him, and shot him dead!'[21]

So writes Miller in his book *Lamp of Lothian,* and adds that the unfortunate man was not present at Tranent at all.

The last of the seven bodies — that of John Adam — was later found at Annfield, near the Haddington road. The Lord Advocate subsequently informed the Home Secretary that Adam's death was a clear case of murder although modern readers may feel that Robert Dundas was being needlessly selective.[22] Certainly, there was evidence that Adam had spent the morning in the St Germains colliery and was unaware of the Tranent meeting and the riot. His death was witnessed from a distance by a fellow collier, and two other unfortunates were involved in the following incident and were later to testify.

Like others who suffered at the hands of the military, Adam was on the road to Tranent, when he met William Tait and Adam Blair.[23] Both had been pursued by cavalry earlier, Blair being cut at the elbow. They persuaded Adam to change his direction, and all three were forced to take to their heels when they saw twenty cavalry gallop towards them. On reaching them the soldiers fired on the trio who either threw themselves aside or were knocked over by the horses, but worse was to come. One or two cavalrymen detached themselves from the main group and one quickly recognised Blair from having wounded him earlier. He struck him again, leaving him for dead. Tait crawled under a nearby cart where he escaped the soldiers' notice, but Adam, probably terrified and unable to understand why this was happening to him, pleaded for mercy.

One dragoon told him, 'there's your mercy!' and shot him. Another soldier mocked him as he lay wounded and when Adam's body was later recovered he was found to have been shot twice in the chest, and cut on the chest, arms, hands and stomach.

These were to be the last of the Tranent deaths indicated in the records, although only good fortune preserved some villagers. Both John Blackie and William Kedzlie were attacked by mounted soldiers, and both heard bullets whistling past their ears.[24] In Kedzlie's case it was reported that the bullets took a piece of ear with them, while Blackie was struck, fortunately without serious injury, by sabre blows. Neither appear to have been involved in the riot.

It would be inaccurate to imply that all the cavalry were bent on wholesale murder. As the *Scots Chronicle* pointed out, some officers were heard trying to recall their men, and there are recorded cases where officers interceded to save innocent lives.[25]

Robert Ross, a Pencaitland mason who had not been at Tranent, successfully appealed to an officer for clemency when surrounded by a group of cavalry.[26] George King, quietly occupied in spreading lime in a field was confronted by cavalrymen who 'damned him for a Scots buggar', and would probably have shot him were it not for the timely appearance of an officer.[27] William Montgomery, a septuagenarian, was told by some cavalrymen — fresh from the murder of John Adam — according to McNeill — that they 'would make a target of him' when an officer appeared to restrain the soldiers.[28]

It is surely more than coincidence that three lives were saved in this manner; more probably, officers left Tranent and rode after the undisciplined groups of cavalry following the failure of the Cinque Ports bugler to recall the Pembrokeshires. It is chilling to think that only a few minutes further delay by these officers, only a few inches deviation in two bullet trajectories, prevented the Tranent death-toll from approaching twenty. As it was, the two cavalry regiments notched up what was probably the largest total of mass-killings in Scotland since Culloden.

How does the historian analyse such an event? Is it possible to guess at the motivation which drove these soldiers to murder unarmed civilians whose connection with the foregoing riot must have been doubtful in the case of those fleeing the village, and impossibly tenuous in the case of those working in the fields or journeying along the roads to Tranent? One characteristic of massacres — from the slaughter of the Macdonalds at Glencoe to the My Lai atrocity in Vietnam — was the feeling of alienation which made the perpetrators of these incidents believe that they were dealing with another race, a species denied human status. Perhaps the Campbells at Glencoe were conditioned to believe that the clan system separated them irretrievably from their countrymen whom they put to death, just as many twentieth-century soldiers have regarded non-combatants as being beneath human dignity. Did the Pembrokeshires and Cinque Ports see themselves confronted by a different race ('damned him for a Scots buggar'), or by a different class, a society of troglodytes where whole families laboured beneath the earth?

But perhaps the Tranent atrocity was the product of fear. The members of the two cavalry regiments may have been mindful of the recent newspaper reports of naval mutineers at Spithead and the Nore, of servicemen who seemed to place concern about their own living conditions above that of the nation's defence. From reading of mutineers attempting to sail one of His Majesty's ships to join a foreign fleet, here at Tranent before the cavalrymen's very eyes were British subjects resisting a call to the colours. Can the soldiers be forgiven for forgetting that comparatively few of the colliers read newspapers, that there must seem little point in defending a nation which allowed so many of its citizens such a wretched existence as theirs?

The Tranent incident took place only five years after the French Revolutionary massacres and these undoubtedly planted a seed of fear in the minds of the upper classes, a seed which grew with the news of each new domestic riot. The Scottish judge Lord Cockburn said of his childhood in the seventeen-nineties:

'If the ladies and gentlemen who formed the society of my father's house believed all that they said about the horrors of French bloodshed, they must have been wretched indeed. Their talk sent me to bed shuddering'.[29]

If, in the words of Froude, 'fear is the parent of cruelty', fear of an unknown enemy rising from the labouring classes of East Lothian may have fathered the massacre of August 29th.

The Lord Advocate was in no doubt:

'It is not surprising that some of these soldiers once let loose upon such a dangerous mob, as deserved more properly the name of an insurrection, should go beyond the strict line of duty, and do more than what in the cooler moment they or their officers would have deemed necessary for quelling such tumult and dispersing the rioters'.[30]

This was in a letter to the Home Secretary the following Boxing Day, and in an earlier letter Dundas stated his fear that the incident was a grim omen of how the forthcoming recruiting meetings might result in the capital and in Midlothian.[31] In the event, his fears were unfounded; whatever caused the explosion of protest at Tranent, the combustible elements were not present at meetings in the Edinburgh area. He concluded:

'The source of this business lies deeper indeed than a militia which is but the . . . pretext for the proceedings of those . . . (who) have already done so much mischief'.[32]

The Home Secretary's grasp of what happened at Tranent seems far from perfect. In a letter of the 4th September, Portland mentioned 'the unhappy affair at Tranent of which two companies of the Sutherland Fencible Infantry made a part',[33] although two separate sources show that the Sutherlands did not reach the village until late in the afternoon.[34]

Whatever the causes of the Tranent riot and its unhappy sequel, there was no avoiding the depressing tally of deaths and injuries drawn up by the parish minister, Hugh Cunningham, in his letter to the Lord Lieutenant, the Marquis of Tweeddale, on 2nd September. This must have been a grievous time for Cunningham, whose wife had died only a fortnight previously.[35] He listed eleven dead (leaving out Lawson whom he accounted as 'dangerous'), with five dangerously wounded, and six or seven slightly wounded. These were the morbid returns for his own area; of neighbouring areas, Cunningham added:

'I believe one man belonging to Prestonpans and another in Upperkeith are slightly wounded, but the return your Lordship will have from these parishes will ascertain the point'.

This letter is doubly important because of the apparent absence of death or burial records for Tranent and Pencaitland parishes at the time — according to the first *Statistical Account,* the poor of the parish were unable to afford to register burials.[36]

It is perhaps debateable if Cunningham's letter had a melancholy effect on the Marquis of Tweeddale, whose recorded reaction to what happened in the largest town in his county reads badly two centuries on. Writing to the Home Secretary on 10th September, Tweeddale said:

> 'Altho the desperate opposition given by the populace to the magistrates employed in discharging their duty prescribed to them by the Act has been attended by circumstances deeply to be lamented, yet I have the satisfaction to think that the good conduct of the magistrates and military officers employed on that occasion has been productive of the happiest effect in putting a stop to that refractory spirit . . .'[37]

The newspapers of the time carried reports that the lateness of the harvest was delaying the start of the shooting season in some parts of Scotland. The *Caledonian Mercury* of 14th September reported:

> 'We hear that many gentlemen have resolved to shoot none (i.e. game) till the crop is cut down, which this season will be at least fourteen days later than usual'.[38]

The harvest had not been brought in at Tranent on 29th August,[39] but larger prey than partridges was shot that day.

Why?

Before going on to measure the shadow which the Tranent incident has cast over Scottish history, it is interesting to study why the riot was much more violent than dozens of others triggered by the passing of the unpopular Militia Act.

At Tranent, the riot's course swung in a pendulum of violence between the supremacy held first by the villagers, then by the military. Only force, it seemed, could be used to loosen the grip the rioters held on the situation. Undoubtedly, the village's topography had a lot to do with this.

> 'The street then, as now, was quite narrow and curved slightly so that John Glen's public house which was almost half way along its length could not be seen clearly by the troops at the east end of the street where they were drawn up and those soldiers posted outside the house were isolated from their commander and their fellows'.[1]

Logue has pinpointed the strategic difficulties under which the military had to operate, with signalling problems particularly prominent. Even more difficult was the necessity of using cavalry in a restricted environment where the opposition was well established in vantage-points above ground-level.

At the same time, the deputies' decision to separate themselves from their military escort, although probably necessary to avoid giving the impression that the officials were expecting trouble, gave the rioters a great advantage. An almost parallel case of soldiers being kept in reserve occurred at Wigtown a few days later. During what the county's Lord Lieutenant, the Earl of Galloway, described as a 'tumult', the deputy lieutenants found themselves 'cooped up, in the court house'.[2] The Earl commented that the disturbance was resolved without violence by the Ross-shire Fencibles who 'showed every disposition to act in support of the deputies'. This incident seems to centre on the civilian officials deliberately separating themselves from their military escort in the unfulfilled hope of keeping the meeting on a low key, then finding themselves dependent on military intervention to control a disturbance which had developed into something even worse than had been feared. In the case of Tranent, after military supremacy was established by using live ammunition, the villagers could be chased easily in open country ideal for cavalry action.

Other factors were present at the Tranent incident to explain its violent nature. As Logue indicates, 'the very presence of troops in such large numbers was unusual'[3] and the officials were not slow to summon even more before entering the village. Tranent was obviously expected to be a trouble spot and it is pertinent to ask the question why.

There seems little doubt that John Cadell's position as one of the deputy lieutenants was a contributory factor in causing the violence. As the local coal-mine owner it is possible that Cadell was effectively the owner of many of the Tranent villagers and his presence as something akin to a recruiting officer was vulnerable to all the usual tensions between workers and their employer. Accounts of the riot given under oath seek to portray Cadell's behaviour at the meeting in the worst possible light, even attempting to hold him responsible for the massacre in the fields. This suggests the paying off of old scores with an unpopular employer.

What probably made matters worse was that Cadell may have been the ultimate authority in the Tranent area at the time. Logue points out that 'in other places it seems possible to argue that there were social pressures restricting the way that opposition was expressed'.[4] One possibility might have been the existence of a traditional channel for complaints to be considered by a local member of the aristocracy. We have already seen how in Perthshire the Duke of Atholl represented a focus for dissatisfaction with the militia ballot; there was no such focal point in the north-west corner of East Lothian.

When the Earl of Winton backed the wrong side during the First Jacobite rebellion in 1715, the subsequent sequestration of his estate deprived the area of a landed patron far enough removed from the day-to-day administration of his industrial interests to offer the workforce a disinterested target for grievances. In the event, with the local employer doubling as recruiting officer, the scene was charged with all the ingredients of confrontation.

It is significant that on the same day, a few miles to the south-east, seven hundred inhabitants of the agricultural village of Gifford publicly demonstrated their opposition to the implementation of the Militia Act. They did this by sending a petition to their Lord Lieutenant and then dispersing peacefully.[5] As the Marquis of Tweeddale's mansion, Yester House, is close to the village, the Lord Lieutenant would be a familiar figure to the villagers, one to whom they could address their complaint. Gifford offers the historian an ideal 'control' for putting forward the theory that the Tranent area, lacking an aristocratic landowner, was left to itself to develop an industrial character. It was not unnatural that industrial conflicts would become dominant in local politics, and that the Tranent militia meeting would fuse any industrial unrest with the same element of resistance to the militia that was demonstrated throughout Scotland.

This poses the question — what were the industrial grievances which may have obsessed the Tranent workforce? It is possible that we shall never know, due to the lack of written records left by the villagers. Perhaps the colliers of the Lothians were conscious that their colleagues in the West of Scotland had been granted better working conditions following the passing of the 1775 Act; or did they simply feel that their state of serfdom was out of step with the times? They may have realised the incongruity of their being called on to fight a nation which had embraced the ideas of freedom and liberty; they may have had the irony of it pointed out to them by the unseen 'mischief-makers' suspected by the authorities.

We have already noted the distrust felt by the working-class towards the principle of a militia. There was the ever-present spectre of service abroad in a fever-ridden land and the prospect of conditions more severe than those experienced by volunteers. An industrial area like Tranent would not supply many clients for an insurance scheme run by the Sun Fire Insurance Company, whereby for the payment of three guineas a man was assured of being able to pay for a substitute in the event of being balloted to serve.[6] The women of the town may have been conscious of approaching hardships if the chief breadwinner of the family was forced to leave home at a time of increasingly expensive foodstuffs. Furthermore, with the village recovering from an epidemic five years earlier, which killed many 'in the prime of life'[7], it is possible that there was already a serious shortage of male wage-earners.

All these factors indicate that the extreme reaction of the Tranent villagers to the Militia Act was prompted by a tissue of individual grievances, some common to other areas, some peculiar to Tranent and its specialised workforce. What seems clear however, is that the authorities expected trouble. There was no shortage of troops both at Musselburgh and Haddington, and the deputies were ready to call on them. Altogether, Tranent was visited by units of the local yeomanry cavalry, two fencible cavalry regiments, and one infantry troop — all within a period of eight hours.

Significantly, there was another community in Scotland where almost the entire population was employed at a company enterprise. This was at Carron, Stirlingshire, whose iron-works represented the birth-place of Scotland's Industrial Revolution. Writing to the Home Secretary on 7th September, the county's Lord Lieutenant, the Duke of Montrose, indicated that he had been apprehensive of how to 'restrain the workmen of that establishment of any irregularity, which is very desirable from their number, and hardy habits'.[8] In the event, Montrose acknowledged the role played by the plant's manager, a Mr Stanton, in preventing trouble. It would certainly appear that such industrial areas as Carron and Tranent were regarded as potential trouble-spots; the former seems to have enjoyed the services of a peacemaker who was sorely missed in the East Lothian village. John Cadell was no such figure, and in the absence of an aristocrat who might have commanded respect, the scene was set for a confrontation between the labouring class and its industrial managers, the latter having better weapons.

To the military officers the Tranent villagers may have appeared as undisciplined and degraded, people whose terrible working conditions had reduced their lives to nothing more than a bitter struggle for survival. To the colliers, the deputies and soldiers may have appeared as robbers licensed to steal from the poor, to take away their young men for a war which seemed no concern of theirs. The balloting lists and the Riot Act represented the trappings of a society which showed itself only when it demanded something from the already harassed workers, giving nothing in return.

Aftermath

The Tranent riot and massacre were followed by a long train of legal proceedings in the High Court and the Court of Session, the second trial lasting the best part of three years. What is surprising, is that those on trial were, in the first case, rioters, and in the second, the proprietors of a newspaper which published a letter on the massacre. The soldiers present at Tranent did not appear in any court.

The first reactions of Scotland's newspapers to what had happened at Tranent were made with one eye on the authorities. The *Edinburgh Evening Courant* which appeared on the Thursday following the incident stated in its report that

> 'eight or twelve were killed on the spot, and several severely wounded. Most of the people killed were known to be active ringleaders.'

It concluded:

> 'We sincerely hope that this unfortunate affair will be a proper warning to the rest of the people to pay due obedience to the law of the land'.[1]

That this information was supplied from an official source is suggested by the *Caledonian Mercury* whose report published on the same day begins 'We are authorised to insert the following account of what happened at Tranent . . .'[2] and the details given differ little from the *Courant's* report. Over in the west, the *Glasgow Courier* of September 2nd solemnly informed its readership 'we sincerely hope that this unfortunate affair . . .'[3]

If all of Scotland's papers had been as unadventurous as this, the Tranent affair might have been dismissed as just another anti-militia riot. It was due to the *Scots Chronicle,* a Radical paper founded the previous year, that the affair received any public notice.

'From the accounts already received, there were ten or twelve killed, and about fifteen or sixteen wounded, many of them dangerously, who are now lying, in the greatest agony, some with two or three balls lodged in their bodies, which, notwithstanding the assistance of surgeons from Edinburgh, it has yet been found impossible to extract.'[4]

Other points mentioned in the report were the attack (perhaps *alleged* attack, in view of Wight's later conflicting evidence) on some of the villagers by a dragoon on the eve of the riot, the murder of a boy 'begging hard for his life', and the arrival of the Sutherland Fencible Infantry in the evening. It relates that no arrests were made in the fields, a fact which the cavalry's behaviour makes credible, but which was contradicted by a subsequent official account.[5] It is a largely accurate report, showing the use of local correspondents. But it was not this article which was to divert the history of the Tranent incident on to a new course. This was done by the paper's publication of a letter from Archibald Rodger, who was ostensibly writing to his wife in Edinburgh. Rodger was the brother of Isabel Rodger, one of the two women killed in the riot. The letter is important enough to quote in full.

'Dear Wife

This comes to acquaint you, that you need not weary for my returning home, for my sister is to be buried this afternoon at 4 o'clock, and I cannot come away till I see her decently interred.

I am sorry to inform you of the cruelties that were committed here yesterday — there were six persons shot dead on the spot, of which my sister was one, and she was shot within the door of a house in the town. The number of wounded is not ascertained; but, I am just now informed, that fifteen dead corpses were this morning found in the corn fields, and it is not known how many more may be found when the corn is cut, as the Cinque Ports Cavalry patroled thro' the fields and high roads to the distance of a mile, or two miles, round Tranent, and fired upon with pistols, or cut with their swords, all and sundry that they met with: Several decent people were killed at that distance, who were going about their lawful business, and totally unconcerned with what was going on in the town. I am informed that this was unprovoked on the part of the people; for they assembled peaceably, by public intimation from the Lord Lieutenant and his

Deputies, to state their objections, if they had any, to the roll; but when they presented their petitions and certificates, they were totally rejected, especially by Mr Caddel (sic), who told the people he would receive none of them, as they were determined to enforce the Act, and as the people insisted to be heard, he, with his own hands, pushed them from the door, upon which some boys and women threw several stones at the windows. The assistance of the cavalry was immediately called for, and ordered to charge, sword in hand, and then followed the bloody business above related. But my hand can scarcely hold the pen longer to give you any further details.

I am, your loving husband,

A . . . R . . .

Tranent, August 30th'

Rodger was probably mistaken in ascribing the massacre exclusively to the Cinque Ports and his total of at least twenty-one dead (six in the village, fifteen in the fields) is unsubstantiated. Accurate or not, this letter must have been political dynamite, particularly as there was a complication we shall see later. In the event, the explosive burned with a slow fuse. It is significant that there was no reaction to it until after October 10th, the date fixed for the trial of the Tranent rioters in the High Court in Edinburgh.

The month of September saw the authorities establish some measure of control over protesting communities enflamed against the Militia Act, probably because newspapers were now carrying advertisements clarifying recruitment conditions.[6] Within a fortnight of the Tranent incident, one newspaper even dared to mock anti-militia rioters, the *Glasgow Courier* publishing a letter purporting to come from Bessy Bell and Mary Gray of Bannockburn, writing 'in the name of the young women of Scotland' and suggesting that those men reluctant to join the militia should be the ones wearing petticoats.[7] The Tranent experience did not prove to be a fore-runner of violence in the Edinburgh area, but the historical sources, printed and private, show that the wound was too tender to be ignored. Writing on the 3rd September to his nephew the Lord Advocate, Henry Dundas, Secretary of State for War, said of Tranent:

'There must be something very special in the case indeed, if I shall
be induced to alter an opinion I have always hitherto entertained
that when Resistance is made to such an extent to call in Military
force they ought to be used as necessary.'[8]

More moderate comment came from the *Scots Chronicle*. Its edition
of 5th September contained a letter signed 'Britannicus' addressing
David Anderson, one of the deputy lieutenants with the suggestion that
he should make a statement to clarify the Tranent affair:

'I am sure then, sir, you will not think it mispent time, that may
be employed by you in giving the Public a genuine account of
those transactions'.[9]

Evidently Anderson was already thinking along these lines. Shortly
afterwards — although the timing is probably coincidental — all four
deputies issued an address to the Lord Lieutenant giving their version
of what had happened.[10] Since the Tranent affair had

'given rise to a variety of false statements and injurious
reflections; we think it is our duty to submit to your Lordship as
concise an account as possible of what happened on that
occasion'.

and their version, which made no mention of the deaths, was
particularly kind to Cadell in describing his efforts to read the Riot Act
and then his foray into the street after the cavalry had begun to clear
the area but before the shooting began in earnest. He was reported to
have

'entreated of the people for God's sake to disperse; but instead of
attending to his entreaties, they assaulted him with showers of
stones . . .'

Although this account may not have been published until the 27th
November, the original letter is dated 8th September. It is possibly
significant that Tweeddale's letter expressing satisfaction with the
soldiers' behaviour at Tranent is dated two days later. Perhaps
Tweeddale accepted his deputies' letter as the 'official' report of what
had happened.[11]

Another contemporary account of the incident, again biased
towards the authorities, was published with the title *Narrative of the
proceedings at Tranent*.[12] This contained eye-witness testimonies of how

the officials and military had been harassed by the villagers of whom 'the colliers in particular were remarkably assiduous'.

Meanwhile, the Marquis of Tweeddale forwarded his balloting lists to the Home Secretary on 5th October.[13] Despite Tranent, this was better than some lord lieutenants were able to do; the Dumfriesshire lists did not reach London until the end of the year. Eventually, East Lothian militiamen, some of whom were recruited so bloodily, were incorporated into the 10th Militia regiment under the command of the Duke of Buccleuch.[14]

The rest of Britain was beginning to realise that something unusual had happened at a place called Tranent. At the Shakespeare Tavern in Westminster the prominent Whig, Charles Fox, said:

'With regard to what happened at the meetings upon the Militia Law (in Scotland) you must be aware I allude to the proceedings at Tranent. I am well assured that the accounts which appeared in the newspapers concerning that affair were very mitigated and below the mark. But they contain enough to excite your horror'.[15]

This speech was made on 10th October;[16] by coincidence the date of the trial of the Tranent rioters at the High Court in Edinburgh.

The records show that the Tranent rioters were not the first to appear in court that day. This befell four of the Eccles rioters who could have had little cheer that autumn morning in facing the formidable duo of Robert Dundas, Lord Ádvocate, prosecuting, and Lord Braxfield, the Lord Justice Clerk on the bench. Their defence was conducted by a certain Walter Scott, whom Logue suggests had little sympathy for rioters.[17] In fact, it was only three years since Scott had been bound over for 'breaking the heads' of three Irish Jacobins in a theatre riot.[18] The Eccles four were found guilty, with Braxfield comparing their crime to that of sedition. Their sentence — fourteen years transportation — would come as no surprise to those knowing Braxfield's record as a judge, and may have produced a recoil effect when the Tranent case followed.

From the bloody events of August 29th, with its thirty-six arrests, only six were summoned to appear. These were David Duncan, Elizabeth or Elly Duncan, John Nicolson, Francis Wilson, Robert Mitchell, and Neil Reidpath. As the hearing opened, only three were present, and this was reduced to two when defence counsel argued successfully that as the woman's name was actually Alison Duncan she was not answerable to the charge. She was released on bail, pending the preparation of a new indictment.[19] David Duncan, Nicolson, and Wilson, all failed to appear and were outlawed. This left Mitchell and Reidpath as the only participants in the Tranent incident to face criminal charges on this occasion. The former was defended by John Clerk, who was later to become Solicitor General, the latter was defended by Scott, not then known as a novelist.

Both men pleaded Not Guilty and were able to justify their presence at the militia meeting as they believed themselves to be over the age-limit for ballotees. A number of witnesses testified to their good behaviour, although in so doing a witness named Brotherstone (possibly related to one of the slain) fell foul of Braxfield and was imprisoned for concealing the truth upon oath.[20] Mitchell argued that he was innocently sheltering in the house of James Irvine when Captain Findlay's sword was thrown in through a window, and as David Duncan, in a written declaration on 31st August, had already admitted throwing it,[21] there was considerable justification for believing that Mitchell had been wrongfully arrested. One prosecution witness claimed seeing Reidpath wearing a blue coat in the crowd, while another had seen him on the rooftops wearing a green one.[22] In fact, he had been arrested by cavalry a mile to the south of the village[23] and was not identified as an active rioter by either Major Wight or Captain Findlay.[24] All this represented an unimpressive legal climax to the Tranent riot which had so concerned the authorities, and this appeared doubly so when the jury returned a verdict of Not Proven the following day. As Logue points out, any jury would be unwilling to convict on such inconclusive and contradictory evidence, especially in view of the sentence imposed on the Eccles rioters.[25]

A complicated footnote to the trial concerned Francis Wilson, one of those outlawed for his non-appearance. At the end of the trial, on the Thursday, John Morthland, whose name will reappear in the aftermath of the Tranent incident, spoke on behalf of Wilson. He claimed his client to have been trebly unfortunate. After taking ill on his way to court for the opening of the trial, a message Wilson sent was delivered too late to prevent his being outlawed, and then his counsel Henry Erskine was taken ill with 'sore eyes'.[26] This explanation was insufficient to lift the charge of fugitation against him, and he was shortly afterwards committed to prison. Logue suggests that Wilson had hidden until the verdict on the other supposed rioters was known, and that the Lord Advocate dropped the case the following year to avoid rekindling public interest.[27] On the other hand, the *Scots Chronicle* reported that the Lord Advocate had intimated Wilson's belated arrival to the court the day *before* the verdict, and it is possible that Wilson's story was genuine.[28]

To the modern reader, the Edinburgh trial of two innocent bystanders at the Tranent disturbance was a poor conclusion to one of Scotland's bloodiest incidents since Culloden. That some of the soldiers giving evidence might have been more appropriately in the dock is not only a modern suspicion; on the 10th October, before the trial commenced, Morthland had written to the Lord Advocate asking whether members of the Cinque Ports Cavalry

> 'some or all of whom may turn out to be murderers of the innocent people, are proposed to be witnesses against the alledged (sic) rioters'.[29]

He did not receive a reply.

Morthland wrote this letter after learning of the efforts being made to bring some of the soldiers to justice, efforts made by Alexander Ritchie, a W.S. with Radical views, and a weaver called William Neilson whose servant Isabel Rodger had died at Tranent. Ritchie and Neilson interviewed a number of relatives and widows of the deceased, taking statements from them. Logue believes that their activities were instrumental in forcing the authorities to publish the *Narrative of the proceedings* in an attempt to allay further dissatisfaction with their handling of the Tranent riot.[30] Certainly the pamphlet seemed geared to tackle the unfavourable publicity the incident had already received, particularly in the *Chronicle:*

> '(A) Report says that some innocent persons suffered along with the guilty; a circumstance which seems by no means improbable, if those persons be called innocent who (if they do not offer their aid in support of the insulted authority of the Civil Magistrate) do not at least keep in their houses, or . . . remove as far as possible from the scene of such lawless and criminal proceedings'.[31]

After receiving a rebuff from the Lord Advocate, Ritchie and Neilson presented their evidence to the Sheriff and Justices of the Peace[32] at Haddington and these statements then found their way to Lord Advocate Dundas for use in a possible prosecution. The Lord

Advocate was disinclined to take such a course of action, and as we shall see later, had powerful reasons for not doing so. In fact Dundas was more prepared to take action against the champions of the Tranent villagers and it is significant that at about this time Ritchie and Neilson's activities were investigated by the Haddington Procurator-Fiscal. Logue relates how an attempt was made to prove that the relatives had been bribed into giving evidence against the soldiers, but the Lord Advocate was unsuccessful in making out his case, which was dismissed as 'incompetent'.

As Dundas did not redraft his charge against Ritchie and Neilson, the modern reader may suppose that Dundas felt he was on very thin legal ice, and that the less continuing publicity the case received, the better. This was also a contemporary suspicion, and it is worth quoting at length a legal statement made by John Johnstone, the printer of the *Scots Chronicle:*

> 'The facts . . . became the subject of precognitions, by authority from the Court of Justiciary, at the instance of the relations of the murdered persons, all of which were laid before the Lord Advocate of Scotland, with a view to prosecutions; but his Lordship, for reasons best known to himself, has never thought proper to institute any such prosecutions; but on the contrary, brought a petition and complaint against Mr Alexander Ritchie, writer to the signet, who was employed in taking the said precognitions for having, as his Lordship was pleased to allege, instigated the unfortunate people to these steps. Which petition and complaint was dismissed by the Court of Justiciary as incompetent; and his Lordship has never thought proper to renew his prosecution of Mr Ritchie in a competent form'.[33]

To those of us living in the post-Watergate age, Robert Dundas's conduct of the case might suggest an attempt at a 'cover-up'. However, by the time the above statement was presented to the Court of Session in Edinburgh in 1799, the Tranent affair had embarked on a new course.

Two months after Archibald Rodger's letter appeared in the *Scots Chronicle,*[34] John Cadell brought a libel action against the paper's printer John Johnstone and its alleged proprietor, John Morthland. The trial papers, which occupy no fewer than eleven volumes of the Court of Session records, show that Morthland began by denying his connection with the newspaper, while Johnstone used a variety of defences. After commenting on the delay between the paper's publication of Rodger's letter and the date of Cadell's law-suit, Johnstone went on to maintain that Cadell's name was to have been removed from the published letter but had been retained through a compositor's error. As to the delay, the defendant implied that this had occurred because the authorities — and Johnstone obviously believed that Cadell had powerful support in bringing his suit — felt denied of their pound of flesh at the October trial with its Not Proven verdict.

As the trial — concerning Cadell's alleged misconduct at the riot — proceeded, Johnstone switched his tactics, and as Logue puts it, 'tried to show that the statement was not only true but that Cadell's behaviour was even worse than the letter said'.[35] Such witnesses as Isabel Smith[36] and Helen Todd[37] testified that Cadell had struck Janet Hogg — this was corroborated by Hogg herself[38] — also, a number of witnesses claimed seeing him throw the first stone of the incident;[39] there was an allegation that he had struck John Farmer,[40] and to cap it all, the massacre in the fields was attributed to an order given by him to Captain Findlay.[41] On the other hand Cadell's behaviour was defended by Alexander Thomson, the Ormiston schoolmaster, Thomas Cunningham, the Tranent surgeon, William Aitchison, the distillery owner at St Clements Wells, and William Dodds, farmer.[42]

In contrast to the brief trial of the rioters, this case, involving the honour of a middle-class industrialist, dragged on for the best part of three years. It ended with a token victory for Cadell, a fine of £300 being awarded against the *Scots Chronicle*. Although this punishment was later quashed by the House of Lords, the paper was ruined. Logue comments that the decision in the Lords suggests that there was probably some substance in the complaints against Cadell whose public standing can hardly have been enhanced by the revelations in the Court of Session, allegations infinitely worse than those made against him in the original letter.[43] Historians must be grateful to Cadell and his anonymous backers for attempting to crush the *Chronicle*, for without this trial there would be even less evidence than that which exists about the massacre.

Another who may have suffered in the aftermath of the Tranent affair was John Morthland. As he was assisting Ritchie and Neilson in their efforts to bring the troops to justice — or at least to court — manoeuverings were being made to expel Morthland from the Faculty of Advocates. Although this movement was unsuccessful, it did not escape the attention of Fox at Westminster who commented 'there may be aristocrats in Scotland, but they cannot in their feelings be gentlemen'.[44]

One gentleman who had a close connection with the Tranent riot and massacre, and the subsequent court proceedings, was Robert Dundas, Lord Advocate. It is interesting to speculate why Dundas did not prosecute those responsible for the deaths at Tranent, and the results of such speculation tell us a great deal about the character of the society in which he lived. He may have considered such a prosecution; this is indicated in his Boxing Day letter to the Home Secretary with its concession that 'Lawson and Adam appear to have been entirely innocent and to have lost their lives most unjustifiably',[45] and by his request to the London lawyer, Baldwin, for an outside opinion on the need for legal action. As we know, Baldwin thought this unnecessary because of the alleged provocation. It would perhaps be unrealistic to expect Dundas to be anything but reluctant to prosecute military units engaged in quelling rioters — only five years previously, on 5th June 1792, his house in Edinburgh's George Square had been attacked by a mob.[46] And there was a further reason for his reluctance to act.

The war with France had drawn a strong patriotic response from members of the British establishment, particularly from those who thought they could hear the rumblings of the tumbrils across the Channel. Many of the upper and middle classes joined volunteer or yeomanry regiments as part-time soldiers in their local area, or served full-time in fencible regiments intended for service anywhere in Britain. Even Walter Scott, lame though he was, became quartermaster to a volunteer cavalry force in Edinburgh.[47] Obviously, if Dundas had decided to bring charges against the soldiers who participated in the Tranent atrocity, he would have to bear in mind the powerful status of their officers, including those not present at the village.

The officers of the Pembrokeshires, possibly more culpable than the Cinque Ports, included no outstanding establishment names, but the Cinque Ports represented a roll-call of eighteenth and nineteenth century celebrities.[48] This should cause the historian no real surprise as the Lord Warden of the Cinque Ports was none other than William Pitt, Prime Minister. Pitt's biographies suggest that he took a strong interest in the raising of volunteer and fencible regiments in his area. One source indicates that he may have drilled troops himself.[49] another that he brought himself to the edge of bankruptcy by spending so much on the training and equipment of Cinque Ports troops.[50] He seems to have been wearied by their insistence on their favoured status and privileges including — ironically — their belief that they should not be made to serve abroad. To this, Pitt is reputed to have commented testily, 'except in case of invasion'.[51]

Knowing Pitt's involvement, it would not be unnatural for up-and-coming politicians to serve in a force so closely connected with their political patron. The colonel of the Cinque Ports Cavalry was Lord Hawkesbury,[52] the twenty-seven year old son of the Earl of Liverpool. At the time Hawkesbury held no major government post, although one source suggests he had been appointed Master of the Mint in 1796, but he had been regarded as a favourite of Pitt's since 1792 and was a keen supporter of the war against France after witnessing the fall of the Bastille to the Paris mob. He was an opponent of parliamentary reform, and had he been present at Tranent instead of Haddington on 29th August, he would probably have been unimpressed by the crowd's complaints against the Militia Act, or their manner of expressing their dissatisfaction. The regiment's lieutenant-colonel was John Hiley Addington, younger brother of Henry Addington, then Speaker of the House of Commons.

Robert Dundas could not have known that Hawkesbury was to become Prime Minister as Lord Liverpool within fifteen years and that Addington's brother would attain that position within five. But perhaps the deciding factor in Dundas's lack of legal action against the Cinque Ports Cavalry was the fact that the major of the regiment was — Robert Dundas.[53] [54]

Major Robert Dundas was the twenty-six-year-old cousin of the Lord Advocate, and the son and personal secretary of Henry Dundas, Secretary of State for War. As M.P. for Rye along with Hawkesbury, the young Robert Dundas was embarking on a career which would take him as high as First Lord of the Admiralty when his then colonel, Hawkesbury, became Prime Minister as Lord Liverpool.

Were the deaths at Tranent important enough to warrant stirring up a furore in government circles, and in one family circle? The Lord Advocate was in an awkward position, even although contemporary sources do not appear to indicate that the family connection was widely known to Dundas's critics. The ruling elite of the seventeen-nineties was probably too insecure and too inter-knitted to withstand the kind of prosecution which Dundas might have felt obliged to prepare, and with the country at war, the Advocate was probably glad to let the matter rest.

If blood is thicker than water, aristocratic blood is thicker still, although this dilemma posed an additional problem. Dundas would have to consider his own political future; the post of Lord Advocate was, and is, a political appointment, and Dundas's future would depend on Pitt's goodwill.

Thus, the Tranent riot and massacre has shrunk to nothing more than a footnote in the history books — an episode in which many questions remain unanswered. As to the rights and wrongs of the incident, it can reasonably be argued that the Tranent rioters represented a real threat to the well-being of the civilian and military officers present and made the intervention of soldiers inevitable. On the other hand, there is evidence that the public meeting was maladministered from the outset, that the Riot Act was not read properly to ensure that the rioters knew that the soldiers were about to fire with ammunition, and in the opinion of the Commander-in-Chief (Scotland), sufficient action was taken in the village to allow the meeting to continue, indicating the needlessness of the deaths in the fields. The final twist in the tale is the Lord Advocate's inaction in failing to prosecute those he believed to be responsible for murder. This is a black mark in Scottish legal history and raises the question of the suitability of the nation's chief prosecutor being a member of the government.

While Scottish legal annals have given the Tranent affair less than its due, British histories are similarly lacking in the attention they devote to the affair. The *Dictionary of National Biography* says of the Home Secretary, the Duke of Portland:

> 'Portland's administration was marked by . . . no outrage worse than trade processions with seditious flags at Sheffield, and the breaking of the king's carriage windows on his way to open parliament, while Lord Sidmouth's administration, in the corresponding period of repression in 1816-22 was signalised by the Peterloo massacre and the Cato Street conspiracy'.

History seems to have forgotten the massacre which 'signalised' the Home Secretaryship of the Duke of Portland.

APPENDIX I

REFERENCES TO LITERATURE

A detailed account of the Tranent Riot and Massacre by Kenneth J. Logue, entitled 'The Tranent Militia Riot of 1797' appears in the *Transactions of the East Lothian Antiquarian and Field Naturalists' Society*, Vol. 14, 1974, pp. 37-61. A more recent account by the same author is contained in his book *Popular Disturbances in Scotland 1780-1815*. (John Donald, 1979).

Other accounts are James Miller's *Lamp of Lothian*, 1844, J. Sands's *Sketches of Tranent in the olden time*, and Peter McNeill's *Tranent and its surroundings*, 1884.

The Reaction to the Scottish Militia Act, 1797

[1] Logue, K. J. "The Tranent Militia Riot of 1797". *Transactions of the East Lothian Antiquarian and Field Naturalists' Society*, vol. 14, 1974, p. 40.
[2] *Edinburgh Evening Courant* (EEC), 12,366, 29th August 1797.
[3] Logue, *op. cit.*, p. 52. Date given as 17th August.
[4] *Caledonian Mercury* (CM), 11,854, 26th August 1797. *Glasgow Courier*, (GC), 938.
[5] Home Office Correspondence, RH 2/4, 80, p. 162.
[6] EEC, 12,366.
[7] *Ibid.*
[8] CM, 11,857, 2nd September 1797.
[9] H.O. Corr., 80, p. 160.
[10] *Scots Chronicle*, 167, 1st September 1797.
[11] *Ibid*, 170, 12th September 1797.
[12] Meikle, H. W. *Scotland and the French Revolution*. Glasgow, 1912, p. 181.
[13] H.O. Corr., 81, p. 55.
[14] SC, 167.
[15] SC, 164, 25th August 1797.
[16] H.O. Corr., 81, p. 53.
[17] SC, 168, 5th September 1797.
[18] H.O. Corr., 81, p. 134.
[19] EEC, 12,375, 16th September 1797.
[20] H.O. Corr., 81, pp. 43-48.
[21] *Ibid.*, 81, p. 86.

[22]   Meikle, *op. cit.*, p. 182.
[23]   H.O. Corr., 81, p. 86.
[24]   H.O. Corr., 80, p. 156.
[25]   H.O. Corr., 81, p. 15.
[26]   Laing MSS, Edinburgh University Library, II. 500. Letter dated 3rd September 1797.
[27]   According to his entry in the *Dictionary of National Biography*, the Duke of York was not appointed Commander in Chief until April 1798. However, as his predecessor, Lord Amherst, died a month before Dundas wrote this letter, and had apparently been encouraged to resign in York's favour in 1795 (DNB), it seems reasonable to assume that York was C in C at the time.
[28]   H.O. Corr., 81, p. 36.
[29]   H.O. Corr., 81, p. 131.
[30]   H.O. Corr., 80, p. 190.
[31]   H.O. Corr., 81, p. 31.
[32]   SC, 172.
[33]   E. P. Thompson. *The making of the English working class.* (1974 Penguin Edition), pp. 73/4.
[34]   Western, J. R. The formation of the Scottish militia in 1797. *Scottish Historical Review,* Vol. 34, 1955, pp. 1-18.
[35]   SC, 167, 1st September 1797.
[36]   CM, 11,865.
[37]   CM, 11,855, 28th August 1797; GC 938.
[38]   H.O. Corr., 81, p. 36.
[39]   H.O. Corr., 81, p. 60.
[40]   EEC, 12,366, 29th August 1797.'
[41]   H.O. Corr., 81, p. 55.
[42]   Barnett, C. *Britain and her army, 1509-1970.* Penguin, 1970, p. 234.
[43]   H.O. Corr., 81, p. 55.
[44]   *Ibid.*
[45]   Western, *op. cit.*, p. 2.
[46]   H.O. Corr., 81, p. 162.
[47]   H.O. Corr., 81, p. 13.

Tranent

[1]   Third Statistical Account, East Lothian, 1953, p. 82.
[2]   *Ibid.*, p. 178.
[3]   *Ibid.*, p. 177.
[4]   *Ibid.*, p. 35.
[5]   *Ibid.*, p. 178.
[6]   Duckham, B. F. *A history of the Scottish coal industry.* Vol. 1, 1700-1815. Newton Abbot, 1970, p. 363.
[7]   *Ibid.*, p. 120.
[8]   Statistical Account — Tranent (1792), p. 88.
[9]   *Ibid.*, p. 88.
[10]   Smout, T. C. *A history of the Scottish people, 1560-1830.* 2nd Edition, 1970, p. 406.
[11]   Statistical Account, p. 88.
[12]   Smout, *op. cit.*, pp. 430/1.
[13]   Third Statistical Account, p. 182.
[14]   McNeill, P. *Tranent and its surroundings.* Edinburgh, 1883, p. 26.
[15]   Smout, *op. cit.*, p. 436.

[16] *Ibid.*
[17] McNeill, *op. cit.*, p. 31. Duckham, *op. cit.*, p. 280, mentions a child being born underground.
[18] McNeill, *op. cit.*, p. 33.
[19] Smout, *op. cit.*, p. 437.
[20] *Ibid.*, p. 440.
[21] *Ibid.*, p. 433.
[22] Duckham, *op. cit.*, p. 303.
[23] Mentioned in Arnot, R. P. *A history of the Scottish miners from the earliest times.* 1955.
[24] Cockburn, Henry Thomas, *Lord. Memorials of his time.* New Edition, Edinburgh, 1910, p. 72.

The Riot

[1] Miller, J. *The Lamp of Lothian.* 1900 edition, p. 146. This appears to be based on evidence given by Major Wight at the Court of Session hearing, 3rd August 1798. (Court of Session Papers, 214-1, p. 49.)
[2] SC, 167, 1st September 1797.
[3] Miller, *op. cit.*, p. 146.
[4] McNeill, *op. cit.*, p. 129.
[5] Miller, *op. cit.*, p. 146.
[6] *Narrative of the proceedings at Tranent, on Tuesday the 29th of August.* (1797).
[7] Miller, *op. cit.*, p. 146.
[8] *Ibid.*, p. 148.
[9] Scottish Record Office. Process Papers, JC26, 292.
[10] Miller, *op. cit.*, p. 155.
[11] Miller, *op. cit.*, p. 146. H.O. Corr., 81, pp. 105-112.
[12] Logue, *op. cit.*, p. 42.
[13] EEC, 12,368, 31st August 1797.
[14] Court of Session papers, 214-1, 11th July 1799. Condescendence for John Johnstone, printer in Edinburgh. (Hereafter Johnstone).
[15] H.O. Corr., 81, pp. 105-112.
[16] Miller, *op. cit.*, p. 148.
[17] Gloag, W. M. and Henderson, R. C. *Introduction to the law of Scotland.* 7th edition, 1968, p. 743.
[18] Miller, *op. cit.*, pp. 146/7.
[19] Map of Haddingtonshire, surveyed by Wm. Forrest, 1799. Edinburgh, 1802.
[20] Scottish Record Office. Book of Adjournal, D49, 1797-1799.
[21] Miller, *op. cit.*, p. 147.
[22] Johnstone, 11th July 1799.
[23] Miller, *op. cit.*, pp. 146/7.
[24] Crowd estimated between 2,000 ad 5,000 in *Narrative of the riot at Tranent.* (*Anti-Jacobin,* no. 2, 27th November 1797, pp. 59-69); estimated at about 300 or 400 by Captain Price, H.O. Corr., 80, p. 242.
[25] Logue, *op. cit.*, p. 43.
[26] Miller, *op. cit.*, p. 148.
[27] Logue, *op. cit.*, p. 44.
[28] *Ibid.*
[29] Court of Session Papers, 214-1, 16th November 1799, pp. 124/5.
[30] Miller, *op. cit.*, p. 152.

[31] Logue, *op. cit.*, p. 51.
[32] Court of Session Papers, 214-1.
[33] Logue, *op. cit.*, p. 61. Names listed.
[34] Miller, *op. cit.*, p. 148.
[35] Logue, *op. cit.*, p. 44.
[36] Miller, *op. cit.*, p. 148.
[37] Process Papers, JC26. Declaration dated 1st September 1797.
[38] Logue, *op. cit.*, p. 44.
[39] Miller, *op. cit.*, p. 149.
[40] *Ibid.*, p. 148.
[41] *Narrative . . . (Anti-Jacobin)*, p. 64.
[42] Court of Session Papers, 214-1. November 1799, p. 127.
[43] *Narrative . . . (Anti-Jacobin)*, p. 65.
[44] McNeill, *op. cit.*, p. 134.
[45] Logue, *op. cit.*, p. 45.
[46] H.O. Corr., 80, p. 242.
[47] Logue, *op. cit.*, p. 45.
[48] Miller, *op. cit.*, p. 149.
[49] *Narrative of the Proceedings* . . . specifically mentions the Cinque Ports Cavalry in this incident.
[50] McNeill, *op. cit.*, p. 147.
[51] Miller, *op. cit.*, pp. 149/150.
[52] [53] [54] McNeill. *op. cit.*, p. 156.
[55] Logue, *op. cit.*, p. 46.
[56] *Narrative . . . (Anti-Jacobin)*, p. 66.
[57] Miller, *op. cit.*, p. 149.
[58] H.O. Corr., 80, p. 242; SC 167, 1st September 1797.
[59] Logue, *op. cit.*, p. 51.
[60] Court of Session Papers, 214-1, November 1799, p. 116.
[61] *Ibid.*, p. 127.
[62] H.O. Corr., 80, p. 242.

The Tranent Massacre

[1] H.O. Corr., 82, p. 267.
[2] Logue, *op. cit.*
[3] Laing MSS, Edinburgh University Library, II, 500.
[4] Map on p. 39, courtesy of *The Scotsman*.
[5] H.O. Corr., 82, pp. 267-269.
[6] Logue, *op. cit.*, p. 47.
[7] *Ibid.*
[8] Miller, p. 152.
[9] Logue, *op. cit.*, pp. 47/8.
[10] *Ibid.*, p. 48.
[11] McNeill, pp. 146/7; Court of Session Papers, 214-1, 16th November 1799, p. 128. Evidence given by Margaret Smith.
[12] Logue, *op. cit.*, p. 48. Cunningham gives Lawson's Christian name as William.
[13] H.O. Corr., 82, p. 267.
[14] H.O. Corr., 80, p. 255.
[15] H.O. Corr., 82, p. 267.

[16] Logue, *op. cit.*, p. 49.
[17] The Pencaitland parish register (Register House, 716/2) does not list deaths or burials for 1797. Neither does it appear to list the baptism of a D. Kemp. William is recorded as having been born on 23rd July 1785, and there is an Andrew Kemp born 24th July 1780, but in the latter case, a seventeen-year-old youth would appear too old to be described as a boy in a contemporary report (*Scots Chronicle*, 167), and William's evidence gives his brother's age as thirteen or fourteen. It must be assumed that William's elder brother referred to as "D" was baptised elsewhere. The fact that he did exist, and was killed at Tranent, is attested by the Cunningham letter of 2nd September, and William's testimony in one of the two subsequent trials. H.O. Corr., 82, p. 281.
[18] Logue, *op. cit.*, p. 49.
[19] *Ibid.*
[20] SC, 167.
[21] Miller, p. 150.
[22] H.O. Corr., 82, p. 267.
[23] Logue, *op. cit.*, p. 50.
[24] Miller, p. 151; McNeill, p. 156.
[25] SC, 167.
[26] Miller, p. 151.
[27] Logue, *op. cit.*, p. 51.
[28] Miller, p. 151; McNeill, p. 155.
[29] Cockburn, *op. cit.*, p. 41.
[30] H.O. Corr., 82, p. 270.
[31] H.O. Corr., 80, p. 248.
[32] H.O. Corr., 80, p. 249.
[33] H.O. Corr., 81, p. 30.
[34] H.O. Corr., 80, p. 242; SC 167.
[35] Fasti Ecclesiae Scoticanae, I, 1866, p. 360.
[36] Statistical Account, Tranent (1792), p. 91.
[37] H.O. Corr., 81, p. 103.
[38] CM, 11,862.
[39] See Rodger's letter, SC 167.

Why?

[1] Logue, *op. cit.*, p. 57.
[2] H.O. Corr., 81, p. 59.
[3] Logue, *op. cit.*, p. 57.
[4] *Ibid.*, pp. 57/8.
[5] SC 167.
[6] CM 11,860, 9th September 1797.
[7] *Statistical Account,* Tranent, p. 84.
[8] H.O. Corr., 81, p. 78.

Aftermath

[1] EEC, 12,368, 31st August 1797.
[2] CM, 11,856, 31st August 1797.

3 GC 941, 2nd September 1797.
4 SC 167.
5 *Narrative of the riot at Tranent.* (*Anti-Jacobin,* no. 2, 27th November 1797, p. 66).
6 See CM 11,857, 2nd September 1797.
7 GC 944, 9th September 1797.
8 Laing MSS, Edinburgh University Library, II, 500.
9 SC 168.
10 *Narrative . . . (Anti-Jacobin), op. cit.*
11 H.O. Corr., 81, p. 103.
12 *Narrative of the proceedings at Tranent, on Tuesday the 29th of August* (1797), 4 pp. (Anonymous).
13 H.O. Corr., 82, p. 209.
14 Western, J. R. The formation of the Scottish militia in 1797. *Scottish Historical Review,* 34, 1955, pp. 1-18.
15 Morning Chronicle, 11th October 1797; SC 180.
16 SC 179; report begins, 'Wednesday came on the trial of . . .', although the Wednesday of that week appears to have been the 11th.
17 Logue, *op. cit.,* p. 53.
18 *Dictionary of National Biography* entry.
19 SC 179.
20 *Ibid.*
21 Process Papers, JC26.
22 Logue, *op. cit.,* p. 53.
23 Process Papers, JC26.
24 Logue, *op. cit.,* p. 53.
25 *Ibid.*
26 SC 179.
27 Logue, *op cit.,* p. 54.
28 SC 179.
29 Laing MSS, Edinburgh University Library, II, 500. Letter dated 10th October.
30 Logue, *op. cit.,* pp. 54/5.
31 *Narrative . . .* (Anonymous).
32 According to Miller, p. 152, John Cadell was a J.P.
33 Johnstone, 11th July 1799.
34 SC 167.
35 Logue, *op. cit.,*p. 56.
36 Court of Session Papers, 214-1. November 1799, p. 131.
37 *Ibid.,* p. 116.
38 *Ibid.,* p. 121.
39 *Ibid.,* p. 124.
40 *Ibid.,* p. 135.
41 *Ibid.,* p. 127.
42 *Ibid.,* various testimonies.
43 Logue, *op. cit.,* p. 56.
44 SC 180.
45 H.O. Corr., 82, pp. 267-270.
46 Omond, G. W. T. *The Arniston memoirs: three centuries of a Scottish house, 1571-1838.* Edinburgh, 1887, p. 231.
47 DNB entry.
48 Militia, Fencible, Yeomanry and Volunteer List, 1797. War Office.
49 Burrows, M. *Cinque Ports.* 1888, p. 248. '. . . he set to work to organize and drill his famous Cinque Ports Volunteers . . .' Although this probably refers to a later

force, raised during the Napoleonic War, it suggests, if taken with other sources (see below), that Pitt was accustomed to taking a close interest in troops raised in his area.

[50]   Rose, J. H. *William Pitt and the Great War.* 1911.
p. 474. '. . . he gave £1,000 in 1793 to start the Dover Volunteer corps and doubtless other sums towards the Fencibles of the Cinque Ports.'
p. 477. 'Later on he felt pecuniary embarrassments, partly owing to his share in maintaining the Cinque Ports Volunteers.'

[51]   *Ibid.*

[52]   Yonge, C. D. *Life and administration of Robert Banks, Second Earl of Liverpool, KG.* Vol. 1. 1868.

[53]   Militia, Fencible, etc., List. (See 48 above).

[54]   Public Record Office. War Office: Returns etc., (WO 13/3736); Muster roll of the Cinque Ports Fencible Regiment 1794-8 records Dundas as R. Dundas Saunders.

APPENDIX II

The Bonnie Lad was Joe to Me
Tranent Massacre

Let King George sing dool on his throne,
    An' yon red-coated minions be
A bye-word an' a warning groan,
    To him wha wad enthrall the free!
But, oh! alack, he'll ne'er come back —
    The bonnie lad was Joe to me —
A madman sodger hack'd him doun,
    As he ploo'd, whistlin', o'er the lea.

For gatherin' in a lawfu' cause,
    To plead their plea like Scottish men,
The tyrants, traitors to all laws,
    Dealt a wide country death an' pain!
O' bluidy day! o' deadly day!
    That I was born their weird to dree —
That wrapt, my lad, in bluidy clay,
    An' beded me wi' misery.

How fairly seemed that Lammas morn,
    How sweetly heard the shearer's sang,
How clear my laddie's lilt was borne —
    The very hills for pleasure rang.
But ah, waes me! baith lilt and sang
    Was changed or night for sab an' grane;
For mithers wailing sad and lang,
    An' for my laddie slain.

Some will bewail a bairnie dear,
    Was shot or butchered in thir sight;
A brither there — a faither here —
    In red wat death gasht grim that night.
An' thou, my laddie evermair,
    Down to the lagging hour I dee,
For that my heart is fou' an' sair,
    Will wither auld still wailing thee.

71

ACKNOWLEDGMENTS

My thanks for encouraging and assisting me with this study go to Ian Donnachie and Ian Wood of the Open University in Scotland, to the staffs of the Scottish Record Office, General Register Office for Scotland, National Library of Scotland, Signet Library, Scottish United Services Museum at Edinburgh Castle, Edinburgh City Libraries, East Lothian District Library, Kent County Library, East Sussex County Library, Public Record Office, Ministry of Defence (Whitehall Library), and to Miss Margaret Marr for giving me a copy of the folk ballad dealing with the Tranent incident.

Thanks are also due to Dr K. J. Logue and Professor T. C. Smout for permission to quote from their respective publications and to Correlli Barnett and Penguin Books for permission to reproduce a passage from *Britain and her army.*